Room to Grow
an Appetite for Life

Room to Grow
an Appetite for Life

by Tracey Gold

with Julie McCarron

NEW MILLENNIUM PRESS
Beverly Hills

ISBN 893224-66-X

Library of Congress Cataloging-in-Publication Data Available

All photos courtesy of the author's private collection.
Text Design: Kerry DeAngelis, KL Design

New Millennium Press
301 North Canon Drive
Suite 214
Beverly Hills, CA 90210

10 9 8 7 6 5 4 3 2 1

For Roby

who never gave up on me

and

Sage and Bailey

who keep me true

Chapter One

In My Own Words

I believe I would have become anorexic even if I had grown up in a small town in the Midwest and never been an actress. My illness was never a "troubled Hollywood teen actor" thing. The pressures that overwhelmed me were magnified because I was appearing on a popular weekly series, but they were the same pressures that are faced by every girl in America. Every young girl is vulnerable to eating disorders in our society.

I went through an awkward late-teenage phase and gained my "freshman 15" (without ever going to college!). When I started to lose the weight, the affirmation I got was overwhelming. Every single person I saw told me over and over how great I looked, to the point that I became obsessed with how bad I must have looked before. I mean, how could I even have allowed myself to walk around in public, much less be filmed, looking so fat? I had thought of myself as always looking fine, maybe a bit more voluptuous with the added pounds. But the steady stream of accolades convinced me that I must have been huge.

The smaller my body got, the more praise I received. I remember during my illness someone commenting on how beautiful I looked. My husband Roby, who was my boyfriend at the time, snapped, "Don't tell her she looks good. She doesn't look good." He knew how thin I was underneath the layers of clothes. Roby more than anyone knew how deadly serious my condition was. But still, everywhere I went, people were remarking admiringly on my appearance. When I eventually started hearing, "You're too skinny. You've lost too much weight," it didn't alarm me at all. These words are not taken seriously in our society. Unfortunately, they are taken as a compliment.

Many people remember reading about my struggles with anorexia nervosa in *People* magazine, or seeing the TV movie *For the Love of Nancy* in which I starred as an anorexic. Others recall seeing my story as a documentary on the E! channel or *Biography*. My story has been told many times... but never by me. I've never had the opportunity to say everything I wanted to, because my experiences were recorded and edited for a certain format, neatly cut and packaged for a feature article or to fit a producer's particular vision. I've seen many versions of my struggle through the eyes of the media, some sympathetic and some hurtful. What I'm ready to do now is tell people, in my own words, about the way I view young womanhood, anorexia nervosa, and my recovery from this disease.

My experiences speaking at colleges and high schools over the past couple of years led me to this decision. Last year my brother-in-law, who is the alumni director and an alumni himself of Lehigh University, asked if I would address a group on their campus about my battle with anorexia. The tremendous response I received and the standing-room-only crowd was a big wake-up call to me. I had young men showing up to tell me that they were concerned about their girlfriends' eating habits. I spoke to girls whose sisters were acting strangely around food and dropping too much weight. Junior high students who lived sixty miles away were driven to the university to hear me speak because their mothers were so worried about them.

Every single person I spoke to told me how helpful it had been to hear me tell my own story and share whatever knowledge I had gained from the experience. I realized that I had an impact that was much more powerful than I had ever known. I've been "recovered" from anorexia for many years, and over the years I've talked plenty about anorexia because I had to. When the tabloids were writing about me every week I felt I had no choice but to respond as well as I could at the time. This was ten years ago, remember, well before the days when printing pictures of skinny actresses and labeling them anorexic became a commonplace feature in entertainment magazines. I was the first young actress to bear the full brunt of the media glare, and it was brutal.

Even back then, in the midst of all of the chaos, feeling like my life was very nearly destroyed, I believed that a greater good would eventually come out of my ordeal. Actually, I have always believed that all things, good and bad, happen to each of us for a reason. Every step I have taken since then has been a positive experience. After I spoke to all of the people who waited patiently to talk to me in Pennsylvania that snowy night, I had a much stronger awareness of how important my story was.

My book is for every daughter, sister, or friend to find some understanding and, hopefully, some real help. I don't claim to have all the answers, but I do know a lot about this disease. I have plenty of knowledge and years of therapy, and of course I underwent the actual experience. I'm writing a book because I've always loved to read and turned to books for answers. For every life experience I've had—from planning my wedding, to what to expect from pregnancy, to the best way to apply makeup—I read up on it. I've gone through life with a stack of books. When I had anorexia it became my mission to find the answers that would save me, but there wasn't much out there at the time. Again, this was ten years ago, before the word "anorexic" was tossed around carelessly and frequently like it is today.

What this book will NOT be is a manual for girls to discover new and easier ways to lose weight. I myself have been the victim of books that tried to help but actually did me great harm. Along with everyone else at the time, I read *The Best Little Girl in the World*. There is an undercurrent of competition that underlies anorexia nervosa... a twisted desire to be the "best" anorexic. Reading a book like that can put dangerous ideas into a young girl's head—the realization that, *Oh, so that's how she got so thin... I could do that!* I know from group therapy how easy it is to pick up tricks from others with the disease—to learn how to become an even more successful anorexic. The last thing girls with an eating disorder need is someone spelling out the ways they lost weight.

While I was writing this book there was a sudden flurry in the press because the actress Christina Ricci was quoted as saying that she had learned how to become anorexic years ago by watching me in the TV movie *For The Love of Nancy*. This remark was painful to me, because I would never want to do anything to further someone's illness. I had, in fact, done everything I could to make the movie non-exploitative.

I do believe that anorexia nervosa is more complicated than watching a movie. I also know that almost ten years ago my knowledge of the disease—like the rest of our society's—wasn't what it is today. When Christina made that remark I realized that there may be other girls out there who will feel that same way. I cannot let this kind of reaction or how it makes me feel get in the way of spreading my message. I can only try to figure out how to make my message clearer. You can't please all of the people all of the time—I learned that the hard way. All I can do is address what happened and say, look, if you took this movie and saw it that way, let me explain why it was made this way, what I personally went through while I made it, and my agenda while I made it.

I wouldn't make the same movie today, though I remain very proud of the work I did. *For the Love of Nancy,* which was a true story based on the life of a real girl, is shown in most schools across the country, and I know it's helped many girls. When you make a movie about anorexia, to get the point across you unfortunately have to show some of the behavior of anorexia. I did my best at that time to fight to keep a lot of the exploitative aspects out, but I couldn't keep everything out.

The things that I chose to show are things that are pretty common knowledge about anorexia nervosa. If you have the most basic idea about the disease you pretty much know the things that were shown in the movie. I was trying to show a realistic portrayal of an anorexic's behavior, but not tricks. And the same goes with this book: I have to relate some of my behavior as I battled anorexia, but I have tried to be very careful to avoid anything that could lead girls to harm themselves.

At this point in my life I have enough distance and perspective to finally put it all together. This book is about what I've learned. It's about self-esteem, self-discovery, and valuing yourself. It's about *real* control, taking charge of your life. It's for the girls I see all the time who walk around with that false bravado: "I'm fine, I'm fine, I'm healthy, I'm not hungry...." I used to say that too. Of course I was hungry. I was hungry all the time. Hungry to the bottom of my soul. Contrary to popular belief, anorexia is not a loss of appetite. Anorexia is not about food.

I want to reach those girls, who I know underneath their words are scared, scared and tired of being sick and having their lives defined by illness. One of the main factors in my getting well was that I was tired of being "sick girl." It had simply run its course. I had to make a decision: either let the disease control my life and be "chronically" anorexic for the rest of my days, or get serious about recovering. I see it all the time: forty- and fifty-year old women who've been fighting anorexia since they were teenagers. Their lives are shackled to their disease. There are many women like this—they're not in a hospital being force-fed through a tube, but their lives are primarily defined by anorexia. It is the overwhelming force in their world that takes precedence over everything and, more importantly, every*one* else. They are controlled and consumed by what they eat, what they don't eat, and the numbers on a scale.

I wanted very much to get married and have children. To *truly* achieve these goals—and be healthy and present enough to enjoy them—I had to learn how to turn my back on anorexia and go on. Even when I was at the very depths of anorexia, I knew in my heart there was something profoundly wrong with me. I think all anorexics do. But it's scarier to try to get better than to stay sick. The fear of getting better wipes away the pain of being sick. The terrible dread of surrendering yourself to the process of recovery is overwhelming. But somewhere deep beneath this illness, a tiny part of your mind stays sane. A little bit of your soul knows that something is terribly wrong and cries out for help.

I have written this book not only for girls who have been diagnosed with anorexia, or those who are starting to realize that their "control" over their bodies and food is getting out of hand. It's my hope that there is something for everyone here—for parents, teachers, boyfriends, and brothers as well. This book is about more than anorexia, just as anorexia is about much more than refusing to eat and losing weight. I want this book to be something girls can pick up and hold, a source of comfort, encouragement and inspiration. I've been on this terrible journey and emerged from the other side. I've been where you are, asking the questions you are asking, feeling what you are feeling. This is my story. I hope it helps.

Chapter Two

A Good Beginning

My mother says I was as "solid as a brick" when I was born in New York City on May 16, 1969 to Joe and Bonnie Fisher, an upwardly mobile professional young couple who worked in advertising. At the time of my birth, we lived in an apartment in Stuyvesant Town on the Lower East Side of Manhattan.

My younger sister Missy was born only fourteen months after me—"Irish twins," or twins the hard way, my mom always said—and we've always been extremely close. Missy was born in Montana, of all places, where we lived for two years when Joe was stationed there in the Air Force. The four of us returned to live in New York when I was three and Missy was two.

My mom and Joe divorced by the time I turned four. It was a devastating ending and bitter split, though I was much too young to understand the underlying complexities that led to it. All I knew at the time was that Joe, who was my "daddy," seemed to be a chapter in my life that had suddenly been closed. Joe became a ghost after the divorce, which left me fearful and uneasy about male figures in general. I think the feelings of anger, betrayal and hurt that resulted from the trauma were buried for a long time, but it was a burden that never completely left me, and later may have played a role in my anorexia.

My mother, newly divorced, found her inner free-spirit. She had been raised in a Catholic home, but committed the cardinal sin when she divorced. That was the one thing you did *not* do when you were raised in a strict Czechoslovakian family, but she had done it. It freed her to start a whole new life; she was still so young— only 26, after all.

I vaguely recall her dating a few men after the divorce. What I remember best is her dates handing a toy to Missy and me and shooing us off, kind of like, "Here you go, kids, now go off in your room and play and don't bother your mother and me." I was *so* happy when she met Harry; he was different. They met at a bar called Brandy's on the Upper East Side, where he played the guitar and sang. They had a real "seventies-style" free love/peace kind of hookup that quickly turned into the real thing. On paper, a disaster—in real life, true love.

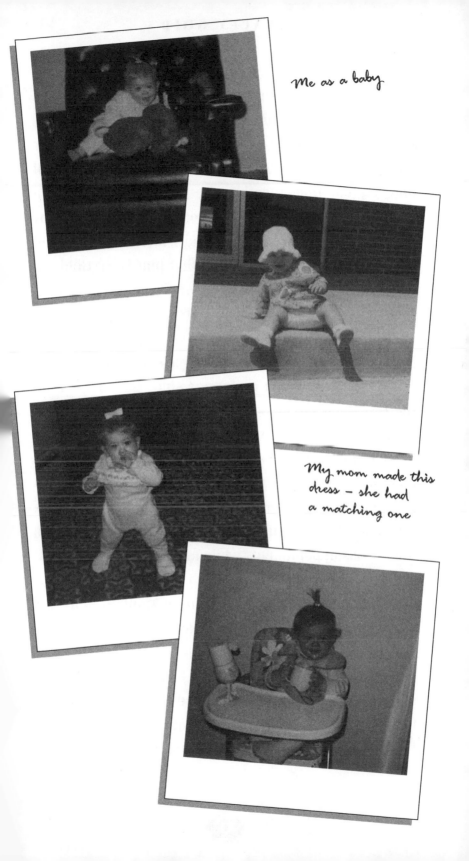

Me as a baby

My mom made this
dress — she had
a matching one

Harry was warm, loving, fun, and also very young—he wanted to play with us when he came over to visit my mom. He was only 21 when they met, six years younger than my mother and only 17 years older than me. We all had a great time together. He was the answer to a prayer for two little girls who were still sad and hurt by the traumatic divorce. Missy and I loved him from the start; he was wonderful. We called him HarryGold, all one word, as in, "Mom, is HarryGold coming over tonight? Can I go with HarryGold?"

Harry was making his living as a singer/actor/entertainer. He had been a performer since he was a kid in the Broadway production of *Oliver* as one of the orphan boys. He performed at night so he was free most days for auditions. As a young girl, I had severe dental problems with abscessed teeth that caused all kinds of complications. My mother had lost a lot of time from work taking me to the dentist, so Harry started taking me to my various appointments while my mom was working at her office. Harry and I spent a lot of time together, traipsing up and down the streets of Manhattan to various dentists and oral surgeons and doctors.

One day, after yet another visit to a dentist, I tagged along with Harry to one of his auditions—this one was for a Pepsi print ad featuring a father and a little girl. I'm not clear on exactly how it came about, but at some point I ended up in the audition with the other little girls getting my picture taken. The next day the casting office called and said, "We'd like to book Tracey." "You mean, Harry?" But it was me they wanted. After his initial surprise, Harry was very enthusiastic. I appeared in that Pepsi print ad. The shot was of a dad hugging his daughter. I had a really hard time with that—the divorce was still fresh in my mind and I was having terrible "father" issues. They wanted me to hug a stranger, and I wasn't about to do it. Finally, in desperation, my mom pulled me aside and said, "Listen. You know those Raggedy Ann Colorforms you've been wanting? We'll get them the minute we leave here if you'll just hug that man!" So I did. And I got my Colorforms.

Then I booked a Lucky Charms commercial. In the commercial I pretended to be a waitress and had a great deal of dialogue for a four-year-old. It was easy for me to memorize my lines and re-shoot the same scene over and over again. Acting was a lot of fun, but it started as more of a lark, not a big part of my life.

We had only known Harry for a year when my mom decided we would all accompany him to California where he was going to further his acting career. By then Harry was "my dad," as he remains to this day, and will be referred to in this book from now on. Our little family packed up and left Manhattan. My dad, a born-and-raised New Yorker, had never learned to drive. He took a few lessons and packed my mom, Missy and me into a '66 Chevy Impala with a hole in its convertible roof. I was five years old.

My parents had very little money when we set out. But we were a very happy family and delighted to be together on this new adventure. We stayed in little tiny motels all through the South and West on the long trip. My parents were thrilled to be starting a new life, and Missy and I were excited to be moving to California. Everything was great. Missy and I had no idea we didn't have much money. We were perfectly happy.

We landed in Malibu at the home of an old-time actress named Fay Spain, who had been a starlet in the fifties. My parents had gotten to know her while they were in Santo Domingo, where Harry accompanied my mom to get her quickie out-of-country divorce. The film *Godfather II* was shot there (it was Cuba in the movie), and my parents got friendly with the cast and crew. Fay, who had a small role, had generously offered, "Come stay with us if you ever get out to California." The kind of thing that's mentioned casually in Hollywood crowds, not usually taken literally. But my parents did.

A year later, we all landed on the doorstep of the incredible beach house she shared with her attorney

Missy and me

Missy and me
in New York

The Wedding —
the invitation
read "Harry,
Bonnie, Tracey
and Missy are in
love, so they're
getting married."

husband Phil. It was right on the sand in a prime area of Malibu—quite a fairy-tale ending to our long journey. Fay and Phil left on a trip right after we arrived, and we house-sat while they were gone. A beach house in Malibu was heaven to our Manhattan family, especially in February. I remember the first time I saw the ocean —I broke out into "This Land is Your Land" at the top of my lungs. Always the ham, and always off-key. It made such an impression on me that I always thought we had lived there for at least a year. I was surprised later to learn that we had only stayed at the beach house for three weeks.

The minute we got settled into our own small apartment my parents found a minister in the Yellow Pages who was willing to marry them without a blood test. It was just the four of us. My dad got Missy and me each a little bouquet to hold while the minister performed the ceremony. They got married because my dad was anxious to start the paperwork to formally adopt us. Though he had become our dad in every way, he wanted to make it official. My parents later had a big wedding ceremony/party at Fay's beach house. Missy and I were the flower girls. During the service we were asked if we'd like to say anything. I said dramatically, "Our life was miserable before we met HarryGold." We were delighted with California and the newfound security Harry had brought to our lives.

The year was 1975, and my parents knew absolutely nothing about Los Angeles. They moved to Lakeview Terrace, not the most desirable neighborhood now but back then, it was much worse—the Sylmar earthquake had just shaken up the area and done a lot of damage. My parents were a free-wheeling, casual, wide-open kind of couple, so they opened the house to the neighborhood and threw a big party when we moved in. My parents gave parties for absolutely every occasion. They still do. Some of our new neighbors gave Missy and me an adorable little dog, which we were very excited about. His name was Elmo (way before Elmo on *Sesame Street*), and we loved him, though he was an ornery little devil. He bit everyone except his old owners. Little did we know that every time we all left the house through the front door, these neighbors would sneak in the back to steal our possessions. The dog didn't bark because he knew them.

I remember returning from a holiday brunch at Fay's beach house on Christmas Day and realizing as we walked into the house that all the presents were gone. They had been stolen right out of our living room. Even the piggy bank Missy and I shared had been shattered and lay on the floor in pieces. However, the straw that broke the camel's back was when we set out one nice Saturday morning to go out to eat and the car was gone. We were all looking up and down the street but it was nowhere to be found. That was it for my mom and dad. No more Lakeview Terrace.

We rented various homes around the San Fernando Valley after that. My dad concentrated on his own acting career, and my parents signed Missy and me up with an agent. Her name was Toni Kelman, and she was a big children's agent. At one time she handled Jodie Foster and all the *Brady Bunch* kids. Toni was an excellent agent—I got my first dramatic role less than six months after my family had arrived in California. I was cast in the biggest dramatic epic of the decade: *Roots*.

I played Sandy Duncan as a little girl and had scenes with Robert Reed, who was a big deal to me at the time. He was the *Brady Bunch* dad! I was thrilled to work with him. I had very elaborate costumes, big pouffy dresses and hoopskirts, and of course *Roots* went on to become *the* television event of the seventies. But what stood out in my five-year-old mind was getting to meet Mike Brady.

Missy and I began to work regularly. I started getting cast in movies of the week in dramatic roles. I did an American Film Institute movie with Mariette Hartley where I had to cry throughout the whole movie. In anticipation of the huge emotional scenes in that movie, the director pulled me aside and told me that

7 years old —
I've worn a crown for
all my birthdays —
I _love_ my birthday!

Baby Brandy

"The Dark Secrets of
Harvest Home" - 1978
That's supposed to be
pig's blood on my hands

Doing "Boomer"
at 10 years old

she had flushed Arnold, my most beloved possession, down the toilet. Arnold was a stuffed bear given to me by a little boy I had met on the trip to California, and I was extremely attached to him. I burst into tears, which was of course the reaction she was trying to get from me. After that I could cry whenever I had to. All I had to do was think of the saddest thing imaginable—at that time, the loss of Arnold—and the tears would flow like water from a faucet. I could now cry on demand, which is a great asset for any actor, but especially a child.

I appeared in many well-made movies of the week with lots of amazing actors. *The Dark Secrets: Harvest Home* with Bette Davis was especially memorable. She played a powerful old witch, the Widow Fortune, and I played the youngest witch. It was a television mini-series based on a popular novel by Thomas Tryon, a horror story about a peaceful New England village where all is not as it seems. It was an excellent production: in addition to the amazing Bette Davis, Rosanna Arquette had the other starring role. Bette Davis was *very much* a grande dame, a diva. That was a little scary to a kid, but she was always very pleasant to me—the ultimate professional. Sometimes I can't believe I've worked with some of the people I now read about, study, and emulate—I was too young to truly appreciate it at the time. The way life works is funny.

Though my sister Missy and my dad and I were all in the same "business," there was never any competition. We all just enjoyed acting and were pleased for each other when we got roles. I don't remember there being any envy or resentment about acting jobs in our family. In fact, I auditioned for *Benson*, the series Missy eventually became very well known on. And she auditioned for *Shirley*, the show I got around that same time. Missy actually got offered *Shirley* and *Benson*, and took *Benson*. I hadn't auditioned for *Shirley*—I was busy working on *Fantasy Island Junior* of all things! When Missy passed, I went in for an audition and got it. This was a series starring Shirley Jones, the mom from *The Partridge Family* (which was a little before my time). Of course, *Benson* ran for seven years, while *Shirley* was cancelled almost immediately. It only lasted one season. I wasn't upset because I was doing a lot of movies-of-the-week, meeting lots of new people, doing some really good work. It truly didn't matter. Not to me at least!

Missy was very well suited to the environment on *Benson* and became famous for her role as Katie, the governor's daughter. I was happy for her. I kept busy—I was getting prominent roles in some really prestigious productions and doing very well. I remember the first time someone said to me, "Aren't you jealous of Missy?" I was taken completely by surprise. The idea of being jealous of my sister had never even occurred to me. I'm serious. I was an actress too, and I worked all the time. Each of us did our own thing. The only thing that ever gave me the slightest pang was that Missy had her clothes on the series designed for her. Since I was a little girl I've *always* been a *big* "clotheshorse," a real "girly girl," while Missy, more of a tomboy, never cared at all about what she wore. Because Missy played "the governor's daughter," she had her own personal designer to design her clothes: the amazingly talented Judy Evans. I was always playing the waif or an orphan, where they'd say to me, "Go roll around in the mud and come back." I literally wore a potato sack in one role! So the beautiful custom clothes, yes, those I envied, but I also got to borrow them. Missy was my best friend as well as my sister and we were always happy for each other's achievements.

I loved having many jobs—moving around and doing different things, while the controlled, predictable *Benson* set was perfect for my sister. Missy liked acting and she was having fun, but she always knew she wasn't going to stick with it forever. Since she was little she wanted to be a doctor. I loved acting. It was all I ever wanted to do, it was in my blood. I was always up for going on location and meeting the crews, staying in hotels, ordering room service. It was all an adventure to me.

My mom and dad split up the duties of watching us. It usually worked out that my dad stayed with Missy and my

mom would travel with me. Having child actors in the
family is a full-time job for one or both parents. Someone
has to take them to auditions and stay on the set with
them while they work. And once they're working consis-
tently, it can really become tricky. It's very important that
you have responsible, caring parents. When a child is making a great deal of money it throws off the family dynamic.
The natural balance of parent and child is inverted.

In my case I was oblivious to the whole matter. If someone had asked me as a kid how much money I made, I
wouldn't have known how to answer. A dollar? Ten dol-
lars? I truly had no idea. Obviously my parents put
aside money for both Missy and me, but we functioned
as a family unit. The money we made as child actors
was used to pay for our private schools and to go on
vacations—Hawaii was our favorite—and other experiences that enriched our childhood and wouldn't have
been possible otherwise.

By this time our family had grown. My sister Brandy
Elise was born in the summer of 1977. Just before she
was born it occurred to my mom what a great birth date
7/11/77 would be, and she did everything she could to
induce labor on that particular day. Instead of floating
on a raft in the pool and baking in the sun, she got up
and did a couple of cannonballs (she was totally nuts!)
into the pool, and sure enough went into labor that

night. My parents named the new baby Brandy in honor of the bar where they met, and her birthday was indeed 7/11/77.

It was thrilling for Missy and me to have a new baby in the house. We adored her so much; we couldn't have been any more excited about having a new sister. Each morning we got up, changed her diaper, made her breakfast, and watched cartoons together. Our family, always close, grew even closer with the joy of a new baby. Baby Brandy.

Missy and I were both working quite regularly and going to school. As child actors, we were required by law to have 3 hours of school every day and a parent or guardian on the set with us. A "guardian" could be anyone who had signed papers for the day agreeing to watch you, but Missy and I always had one of our parents with us.

We were very fortunate... on a lot of jobs we did, we saw that many of the other kids had "guardians" with them. There were always a bunch of kids on the sets by themselves in an atmosphere of tremendous freedom. I always had my mom around keeping an eye on me. She kept me in line. It was work, and my mom insisted on professionalism. I had a work ethic that I think a lot of kids didn't. Most kids thought this was just fun, a kick.

Even when I was six, seven, eight, I realized this was *work*, a job in an adult environment, and I wanted to be the kid people could count on. I was always dependable, reliable, knew my lines. I'd always be the one the producer and director loved because I was prepared and ready to go. They sang my praises, and I ate it up. It was very rewarding to me to be the perfect child actress.

This desire to be perfect, this need to please everyone, was part of my personality probably from the time I was born. (My mom said that on the first morning after bringing me home from the hospital, I slept until 10:00 a.m. Always eager to please.) I loved it when I received praise for being so professional and well behaved. Certainly this part of my personality goes hand in hand with what came later. I thrived on all the affirmation and always strived to be perfect. My mom was a strict mother. She was, and is, wonderful and loving, but on a set there was no fooling around: "We are at work, Tracey," she would remind me, "You are working with adults and you are not going to goof off and fool around. We play at home." I always listened and tried to be the best.

This attitude did a lot for my reputation. I became known in the industry as a well behaved, always-prepared child and got all kinds of work. I did *The Incredible Journey of Dr. Meg Laurel* with Lindsay

Wagner when I was eight. I had to perfect an Appalachian accent and was trained by the renowned dialect coach Robert Easton. My character was stung by bees at one point in the story, so I stood without moving in my potato sack while 100 frozen bees were carefully applied to me, then went ahead and did my scene. Things like this never fazed me—I thought it was all totally, extremely exciting.

I did the film *Child Stealers* with Beau Bridges and played Blair Brown's daughter. We shot that on location in Arizona around Christmastime. It was great. I was in my element… traveling around, staying in hotels, working on different movies. A movie of the week is shot in three weeks, not enough time for anything to become a grind or boring.

I worked all the time. It was a different era in television. Even though there are more networks now, and presumably more acting opportunities for kids, I grew up in the age of the TV movie of the week. There were television movies on all three networks almost every night of the week, and they were *events*, of very high quality. Genres are different today… a lot of the work has shifted to cable, and a lot of television movie roles are filled by movie stars. Back then I was going on six auditions a day—two commercials, an episodic, and a movie of the week. There was that much work.

I got to play Marilyn Monroe as a child in the acclaimed miniseries *Marilyn: The Untold Story* based on Norman Mailer's novel. It was funny, because my sister Missy was the most beautiful blond, blue-eyed child. She had the look you would imagine Marilyn Monroe had as a little girl. When she went to read for the role the casting agent told my mom she was great, but they needed someone with darker coloring, more like mom's: sandy-blond hair and brown eyes. My mom said, "I've got someone right at home for you." They brought me in and I read and got the part. Marilyn had such a sad and traumatic childhood; it was a very emotional role. I've always loved the fact that I played Marilyn—even if it was before she got boobs, blond hair and a nose job. You take what you can.

I flourished when I had to break down and cry. After a very moving scene the producers sent roses to the set to thank me for such a great performance. This was the kind of approval I lived for. I was ten years old.

Television series are shot from August through March. Even though I was a busy working actress, I attended regular school. I would be gone for three weeks shooting a movie of the week, then back in school for a while, maybe missing a day here and there to do a commercial. School for me was in and out, and I did my best to keep up with things. It was easy in elementary school, probably because at that age you're in one class all the time. I had been attending the same elementary school since first grade so I managed to keep up. It was just the regular neighborhood public school near my house in the Valley. My parents never wanted to put Missy and me into a professional children's school. They were of the opinion that kids didn't get the education they needed in that type of environment because the teachers let everything slide so the kids could concentrate on their careers. They wanted us to be regular kids, and in the most important ways we were.

Chapter Three

A Rough Patch

My family settled into a quaint Cape Cod-ish house in Northridge, a San Fernando Valley suburban community. My parents had a room with baby-blue wallpaper built over the garage for Missy and me. Brandy's nursery was hand-muraled in Disney characters by a friend of my mom's. Arnold even got his own special place of honor on the wall.

I had always been a happy-go-lucky kid, except for the time around the divorce when I was prone to temper tantrums. Otherwise I had never taken things too seriously, but something in me shifted when I turned eleven. I'm not sure what brought this change on, but my problems started with a bad bout of insomnia that lasted for about a month. I couldn't fall asleep at night and began to fear nighttime. I remember one day when I was leaving in the afternoon my teacher said to me,

"Have a nice evening," and her words frightened me. Nighttime was scary... it meant I had to go to bed, where I would lay awake all night, tormented by fears I couldn't name. It got so bad I would end up having to go into my parents' room in the middle of the night because I was so afraid, which got quite annoying for my dad. He would go into my room to sleep, in my little twin canopy bed. I couldn't articulate what I was so afraid of; but the fear that I had forgotten how to sleep hung over me.

I was entering adolescence and my body was preparing to change. My nights of insomnia started to ease up a little. I had just completed work on an after school special with Ricky Nelson where I starred as the main girl. When I wrapped that up I went back to school for the last few days before Christmas break. I usually dreaded going back to school, but I was looking forward to all the Christmas festivities. So I returned without making a fuss.

On the Friday before Christmas, which was the last day of school for the year, my dad picked me up after school as usual. I was looking over material for a couple of projects—one was the final callback for the movie *Shoot the Moon*, and the other was a *Hart to Hart* guest spot audition. We were headed to both that very afternoon. As I

Christmas 1980
– post accident

"Shoot the Moon"
San Francisco – 1981

65 stitches!

Viveca, Tina,
Me, Missy and
Brandy – 1981

read my lines to myself, out of nowhere a car broadsided us a block from my school. I never even saw it coming. I was knocked unconscious and wound up needing sixty-five stitches in my face. It was a terrible, serious accident. The car was totaled. My dad escaped injury because the car had rammed into my side, into *me*.

Despite the horrible accident it was a very happy holiday season. I was in the hospital overnight, and when I got home the holidays held an even more profound meaning for us than usual. I was resting at home when the casting people from *Shoot the Moon* called my agent to see how I was doing. My agent told them that I was doing pretty well, that I would eventually be fine, but they weren't sure how my face was going to heal because the stitches were still in and my face was all puffy. "Does she still want to come in and read for us?" they wanted to know. Of course I did. So I went in and read with my face swollen up like a balloon. I got the part, which was a real testament to Alan Parker, the director, because no one knew how I was going to look. But his philosophy was, "Kids get hurt all the time. They have cuts, scrapes, they're not perfect. In my movie, it doesn't matter if she has a scar on her face."

We left for San Francisco for a three-month shoot. They took the stitches out a couple of days before I left. Mom and I went to San Francisco with Brandy, while my dad and Missy moved into our new family house in Chatsworth, another outlying Valley suburb. I got very close to the other girls who were in the movie: Viveca Davis, Tina Yothers (who went on to *Family Ties)*, and Dana Hill. Dana was older than the rest of us girls—she was sixteen. Viveca and I were eleven, and Tina was only seven. Tina spent most of her time with her father, and Viveca's grandmother was there to keep an eye on her. My mom, no surprise, was the strictest adult there. The other girls, who had no previous acting experience, had free rein to kind of goof off.

We spent the first five weeks of the shoot in a hotel, until all the parents got together and protested that it was impossible to keep all these kids cooped up in hotel rooms any longer. So we all moved into the most beautiful, brand-spanking-new apartment complex in Marin County. Those apartments were gorgeous.

At the hotel all the girls stayed in their rooms and played after work while the parents trooped down to the dining room for dinner every night. I wanted to stay behind with the other girls and fool around but my mother wouldn't hear of it: "You have to work tomorrow, Tracey. You need to eat dinner. You're staying with me." So every night I was the only kid who had to eat dinner with all the parents. Making this movie and spending time with these girls was the first time I ever heard the word 'diet' pertaining to me. It was the first time that concept was introduced to me—that kids could diet. The girls' idea of dieting was not to eat dinner, but have a Kit-Kat instead. I mentioned this to my mom, saying something like, "I don't want to go eat with you... I'm going on a diet." My mom said this was complete non-sense and insisted I come eat dinner with her. She was right, of course, but the idea had made its way into my mind. I was jealous of the other girls, who got to roam freely in the hotel halls while I was stuck eating dinner with the adults.

My mom absolutely said and did the right thing where I was concerned, but she didn't always practice what she preached. As a kid I always knew my mom had an eating disorder, though I didn't think of it in those words or in those terms. Missy and I were always just sort of hazily aware that something was a little off with our mom and food. We knew she threw up a lot. She disappeared during meals or afterwards; she very rarely sat with the rest of us and ate. She cooked us great meals but would make herself a little sandwich while the rest of us enjoyed her dinner. Or she'd serve her own tiny portion on a little salad plate.

It was lots of things like that. My mom is only five-foot-two, and she was always pretty thin the whole time I was growing up. She was never anorexic, but she did get very skinny at times. My dad obviously didn't like the throwing-up. Sometimes he would pull her aside and talk privately with her. But this odd behavior was really more of an annoyance than anything else. Yes, he was bothered by some of the things she did, and at times I heard him call her on it, but he wasn't really aware of what a serious problem it was. My mom's message was unintentionally mixed: *You're going to sit down and eat, but I'm not.*

Shoot the Moon was one of the highlights of my professional life. It was an incredible privilege to work with the amazing talents that were assembled for that film: Alan Parker (whose movie *Fame* was in all the theaters and a big hit when we were shooting), Albert Finney (I didn't know who he was, but my mom clued me in), and Diane Keaton (who was just the most wonderful, down-to-earth person you could ever hope to work with). The film was a family drama about a couple with four daughters who split up and the effects on their lives and that of their four girls. To be in San Francisco in the springtime, in the early eighties, with such an outstanding cast... for a kid actress, it was phenomenal. It was the experience of a lifetime. The shoot lasted from January to April, and I hated to leave.

When my mom, Brandy, and I returned to Los Angeles after the movie wrapped, we were returning to a brand-new house in Chatsworth. The house was newly constructed—no landscaping, no curtains, and it wasn't decorated. It had all white walls—to this day, I hate white walls. I had been on this magical, wonderful adventure for three months and was suddenly dropped with a thud into an unfamiliar, unfinished house, thrown back into school and everyday life. I freaked out. I missed my old house terribly and my beautiful baby-blue room, which I would never see again. All my things were in my new room, but they didn't look right. Missy and I now had our own rooms but inevitably ended up in the same room every night. Nothing in the new house felt right to me.

At that time Chatsworth was—and to a certain extent still is—considered way out in the suburbs of Los Angeles. It was off the 118 freeway in completely undeveloped horse country—and we didn't even ride horses. Our new house was one of the first on its block and when we moved in, it was surrounded by empty lots. I was completely shell-shocked, and remember, I was a kid who had moved around a lot. I had lived in two apartments in New York, a house in Montana, and four houses in Los Angeles by the time I was eleven. This new house in Chatsworth was my parents' dream house, the house they meant to settle in for good.

Moving one more time shouldn't have thrown me like it did, but I was just not adjusting well.

I had completely missed the entire moving process. I'd left my house one day to go to San Francisco and work and when I returned my father and Missy were all set up in this new place and accustomed to it. When I left, the Christmas tree was still up; it was April when we returned to the new house. I hated the new house and neighborhood. I was disoriented, even though I had known we were moving for a long time and had seen the house being built. Suddenly it looked ugly to me. Depressing.

My parents were having their own troubles. This period was the roughest point in their relationship to date. My dad was very unhappy with the way his acting career was going. His dream of being an actor, and being able to take care of his family, was simply not coming to pass. He was approaching thirty, and he had a wife and three daughters to support. At five-foot-four, he wasn't a typical leading man, and he didn't look seventeen anymore either, the way he had all through his twenties. He no longer fit into the cute sidekick/best friend kind of role he had played for years.

Acting is a notoriously tough profession, and though he'd worked on a number of big films and series, as the years passed the work was starting to dry up. There were so many times he came so close to real break-through success and just missed it. It had become more and more frustrating, and the uncertainty made him and my mom miserable. It was a tense time in our household as my parents held long, sometimes heated and loud discussions about the future.

I went off to do another movie in June and missed my sixth-grade graduation ceremony from the elementary school I had attended since I was seven. I was shooting *A Few Days in Weasel Creek* with Mare Winningham. On this shoot I particularly noticed that a lot of the actors on that set would go out at night but wouldn't eat dinner. We'd all go out and I would eat, but no one else would. When I'd ask why they'd say, "Oh, I'm on a diet... it's not good to eat at night." I wanted to go along with the crowd and asked my dad, who had accompanied me on location this trip, why I had to eat when no one else did. My dad was exasperated by this. I was twelve years old, what did I know? What I knew was what I saw. Everyone else in my profession did not eat dinner. That was what I was learning.

When we returned home my body started to change. I was starting to develop breasts, and it completely threw me off guard. I was simply not prepared, not able to deal with it. I associated these unsettling changes in my body with getting older, moving out of the house, leaving the ease and carefree times of childhood behind. Becoming a teenager meant moving out of my safe haven. Though I spent much of my time acting, surrounded by grown-ups in an adult working situation, I was treated like a child at home. As mature as I was on the set, when I went home I was an average kid. When the other girls in sixth grade were hiding in closets and kissing boys, I was still playing with my Barbies. I was very much a little girl at heart, in no hurry to grow up.

I had two sisters I adored. Making movies and going on auditions was a whole different world. When I came home I left that work world behind and played imaginary games with my sisters. One of our favorites was a great game we invented and called "Alley." Brandy was Alley, and Missy and I would rescue her from all sorts of different adventures. My parents and Missy and Brandy were my best friends. I never really had any other close girlfriends. There were girls I was friendly with in school, but Missy and I were inseparable. We understood each other, the kind of life we led, the whole acting experience. Our family was different from everyone else's family. We were a bit of a hippie family in the sense that my parents were a little looser and more open with us than parents in the other families we knew. There was never the feeling of, 'You're the children and we're the parents.' It was just understood that 'We're a family, a team.'

For instance, I was never sat down and told about the birds and the bees. I just always knew. These kinds of things were openly discussed around our house all my life. On the flip side, I believed in Santa Claus until I was ten years old. It was heartbreaking news to learn that he wasn't real. I guessed that meant there was no Easter Bunny either.

I had a very close bond with my mom. We looked alike, had similar personalities, and enjoyed doing the same kinds of things. We had spent a great deal of time together on location in hotel rooms and on sets. I'm not sure where I'd gotten the irrational, but very powerful, idea that once you got boobs that was kind of it—you were separated from the family and it was time to go off into the real world on your own. But the concept of being on my own, away from my parents, frightened me terribly. As a result of these feelings I started limiting what I ate.

It was a very "little-girl" way of trying to stop the unwanted changes in my body. It wasn't about being skinny, because I was already skinny. What I wanted to do was stop developing. I wanted to stay a child. My

Best Friends

13 years old –
those bangs took
forever to grow out!

Anorexic the first
time – 1981

13 and weird

personality changed dramatically around this time too. I became more isolated and introspective. I had always been a bit of a clown as a kid, not afraid to look stupid. When I embarrassed myself I never cared; in fact I thought it was really funny. But I suddenly became very self-conscious. I could no longer laugh at myself and be a silly, goofy kind of girl.

These abrupt changes in my personality made my parents realize that something was really wrong with me. That summer that I turned twelve was a tough time. I insisted on dressing like a real little girl and would only wear my hair in two braids, topped by a goofy hat that had either a bear or a whale sticking out of it. Yes, a whale. (During my second bout with anorexia, I made sure not to lose my fashion sense.) By the time July rolled around, when we had our yearly physicals, my parents were very concerned. I wasn't eating and I was really skinny, serious, quiet and sullen... their sunny little girl had disappeared.

During that same summer, I saw the television movie *The Best Little Girl in the World* starring Jennifer Jason Leigh, who I had worked with the year before playing her little sister in an after school special. I remember watching the movie and finding it both appealing and scary at the same time. Years later, when I starred in my own TV movie about anorexia, I wanted to be sure that I avoided whatever it was that made anything about the disease seem attractive, compelling, or in any way seductive.

The movie was based on the book of the same name: *The Best Little Girl in the World.* I had read the book too. It was a very popular paperback at the time. I think any time you see a girl carrying or reading that particular book you should take note because there arc so many hidden messages in it about how to become anorexic. I became obsessed with it, to the point where if my parents saw me reading it they got really annoyed. That book was a bible for eating disorders. Though I'm sure it was unintentional, the novel glamorized anorexia and made being too thin enticing, appealing.

Again, skinniness wasn't the issue with me at this point. It was not wanting to grow up, the desire to remain a little girl. When I went to the doctor for my physical he said flat out, "It looks like she's got anorexia nervosa." I had grown four inches and lost six pounds in the year since he'd last seen me. But he reassured my parents that my illness was in the early stages, and I was still really young.

My physician was Dr. Gettelman, who was also the doctor of Lucille Ball's son, Little Ricky. In one of the *I Love Lucy* shows you can see Lucy running around screaming "Call Dr. Gettelman!" He's in his nineties now and long retired. Back then he was the kindly older doctor, reassuring, a wonderful caring man. He spoke to me privately, and it was like talking to my grandfather. He referred me to a therapist who I saw a few times. The therapist believed, correctly, that the move had really traumatized me. I had never really said good-bye to my old room and my old house. It had been too abrupt, too many changes at such a tenuous age.

I think that these brief therapy sessions were helpful. But I also hated how upset my parents were about my health and wanted to make them happy again. I started to look around and see some good mother/daughter relationships. I realized that you could get older and still stay close to your mother. I started working on a project starring Linda Lavin. It was directed by John Erman, a very famous television director, and he was just so nice to me. He took me under his wing. He respected my talent and abilities and I, in turn, adored him. Working on this movie really helped me over this rough patch, it nipped my eating disorder in the bud. Working with John was such a great experience. It got me out of my dark mood and focused back on work, which I could always count on.

I had a scene at one point in a nightgown. I looked down at my chest and thought *Hmmm… it's starting again.* I told myself, *It's OK, I can handle this. It's not that big a deal.* I was eating and feeling all right again. The crisis had passed…for now.

Chapter Four

Growing Pains

Aftfter this big bump in my life everything started going smoothly again. I was small, but not itty-bitty, abnormally thin. School, on the other hand, was becoming an issue in seventh and eighth grades. I was struggling.

Junior high is where I started to feel the strain of keeping work and school in balance. There's tremendous pressure on kid actors to keep up your grades, because anything below a C- meant you wouldn't get your working papers. Working papers were reviewed and reassigned every six months. Let's say you got a D in the fall and your working papers expired in November. You could not get another set of working papers until your next report card was issued showing a better grade.

None of this had mattered in elementary school, where the work was easy, but the pressure got very intense in junior high. I was constantly worried about my grades.

When you went to the city to apply for your new set of working papers you had to show them your most current report card. No D's, F's or Unsatisfactory marks allowed. That's why many kids who worked as actors went to the kind of school where the teachers would let you slide. My parents, however, remained adamant that we would not attend that kind of school.

I would study really hard, but inevitably I'd go in to take the test and get a D or an F. My parents mostly saw me on a set, where I was smart and on top of things. They thought I was just being flaky, goofing off at school. They got very upset about this; I would get in a lot of trouble—really the only trouble I would ever get into as a teenager. It was a big issue with my mom. I dreaded bringing home bad grades to her, because she would really get mad. She was determined to raise us to be smart. "Nothing worse than a stupid woman," she would tell me, "Nobody wants that."

I was at a loss. I didn't know why I couldn't perform well at school. It only aggravated the situation to have Missy at the same school being so close to me in age. She could do her homework in the car listening to the radio and get straight A's. She was in advanced algebra while I was still stuck in pre-algebra (or math for idiots). I was studying long hours, but I just couldn't make those grades. I didn't know what was going on. I was also working hard doing lots of on-screen projects, and this coming and going in and out of school didn't help.

For eighth and ninth grades my parents had put Missy and me into a little school down the street from our house called Chatsworth Hills Academy. Classes were very small, with only about ten kids in each graduating class. In ninth grade, the year I was fifteen, my work schedule slowed down. Surprisingly, I did pretty well grade-wise that year. Not working such a frantic schedule certainly helped, plus I had more time to socialize and make better friends with my classmates. It was the best year I ever had in school, socially and academically. I graduated with my class and prepared for high school.

Just before I entered the tenth grade I worked with Annette Funicello on an after school special. It was fine— it was a cute production, but I noticed that I wasn't getting jobs like I had when I was a child. I was a different age, going out for different roles. Not a little girl anymore.

That same year I did a feature film with Robin Williams and Kurt Russell called *The Best of Times*. There was a whole subplot where Kurt Russell's son—played by Kirk Cameron, by the way—had scenes with his group of friends. The whole "kids" subplot I was part of wound up being edited out. My scenes landed on the cutting room floor. I did a lot of waiting around—it was a completely disorganized set. It was a whole different experience from doing television. I had only been on one feature movie set before: *Shoot the Moon*, which had been the crème de la crème. The scheduling this time was a mess: I spent hours at a time just sitting waiting to be called. It wasn't nearly as much fun as my first movie had been, but at least there were kids my own age to hang out with while I waited.

Shortly after that movie wrapped, on November 21, 1984, Jessie Lynn Gold was born. She was my third sister and had been a long time coming. My mom had tried unsuccessfully to conceive for two years before she finally got pregnant with Jessie. My mom and dad finally went to an infertility specialist for help, with their three kids in tow, getting odd looks from the other women in the waiting room, who were trying for just one.

Having a new baby sister at the age of fifteen brought out my budding maternal instincts. I was in the delivery room when she was born and cut the cord while Missy clamped. Jessie immediately felt like my baby. She was a perfect little blond, blue-eyed girl who resembled Cindy Lou Who. I loved carrying her around, getting disapproving looks from people who thought she was mine.

Shortly after Jessie's birth I auditioned for the new television series *Growing Pains*. I knew Kirk was audi-

First Crush –
Rick Springfield
– 5/16/83

The Golds – 1985

Mom and me in
Hawaii – she's
pregnant with Jessie

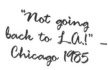

"Not going
back to L.A.!" –
Chicago 1985

tioning for the role of the brother. He wound up getting his role and I didn't. Soon after this my little sister Brandy, who was now seven, was cast in the film *Wildcats* with Goldie Hawn. Brandy was—and still is—beautiful. She was the Gerber baby when she was eight months old, and did a few acting jobs here and there. Missy was still on *Benson*, about to enter its final season. The whole family flew to Chicago where *Wildcats* was shooting on location to visit Brandy and my mom on the set. We made a nice long family vacation of it, seeing all the sights of Chicago.

My dad could only stay a week before he had to get back to work, but the rest of us planned to stay for a full two weeks. Harry Gold had a busy new career. He had come to a crossroads and, after a lot of soul-searching, had finally decided to answer an ad for a job at a small agency, one that represented composers. The decision to become a talent agent was final; there was no turning back. Unlike a producer or director or writer, an agent cannot legally accept acting jobs—it's a conflict of interest. Taking this job meant giving up his dream and heading down a completely unknown path. It had been a life-changing decision for him.

Being in the business as long as he had, my dad naturally knew many actors who weren't represented or were poorly represented. After he got his feet wet in the business he started luring them over to his newly-formed talent division. He had a real knack for agenting, and within a year had his own list of clients—the nuts and bolts of a real business. A year after he began his career as an agent he opened his own talent agency. Though he started out only representing adult actors, a couple of top kids' agents, Ruth Hanson and Joy Stevenson, soon joined him and he opened a kids department too. So he was now my sisters' agent and my agent—though he didn't handle us directly—as well as our dad.

While we were enjoying the Windy City my dad got a call from his office that they were re-casting the Carol Seaver role in *Growing Pains*. Did I want to come back and re-audition? I said, No way. We were on vacation, having fun. Forget it, was my feeling. They'd already seen me and hadn't liked me. Why go back?

My dad said, "Come on, honey. I'll tell them to keep looking this week, that you're not coming home now. If they haven't cast it by the end of the week I'll tell them you'll fly back with me."

I agreed to that, because I knew the role would be cast by then. Of course they'd find someone. But of course they didn't. I was going home early—my plan had backfired.

When a television pilot is shot, each character is test-ed. Each individual character receives a score, and if any one character's score is too low, a lot of times the producers will recast that character. It's tough when you're the one being replaced, but that's the way it can go on a television series. Believe me, I know—I've been on the other side.

When I was eleven I had done the pilot for the series *Gimme a Break*, the sitcom starring Nell Carter that ran for years in the mid-eighties. The producers were think-ing of re-casting me and actually had me audition for my part again, against other girls. This process went on for eight nerve-racking months, while they made up their minds if they wanted me or not. Ultimately, they decided to go with another actress, which was hard at the time. But sometimes things happen for a reason. If I had stayed on *Gimme a Break* I wouldn't have been able to do *Shoot the Moon* or *Growing Pains*.

The first time I had auditioned for *Growing Pains* I had long hair. I was in a real girly, cutesy phase—wearing pink dresses and Mia shoes, even in the snow at Big Bear ski resort—but the character they were casting was Carol Seaver. They were looking for ABC's brand of a nerd; that is to say, the television version of a nerd, and the original actress had been a more intellectual-looking, serious kind of girl. That's not me—the perfectly straight, brainy kind of teenager—so I could understand why I hadn't gotten the role.

Pouting the whole way, I flew back home with my dad. The producers liked me, but said I sped through my audition. There were a lot of long words in my dialogue, plus I talked very fast anyway. (I still do.) They decided: "We'd like to see her one more time, but she needs to slow down." They had the director John Pasquin, who went on to direct Tim Allen's movie *The Santa Clause*, work with me. He sort of fine-tuned me a little and slowed me down a bit before I met the network for final approval. The character Carol was supposed to be thirteen and I had just turned sixteen, but I always looked young for my age.

In the time between the first audition and the second audition I had cut my hair short. I had seen *Ladyhawke* starring Michelle Pfeiffer just before she got really famous. In that movie she had the cutest little blond pixie hairdo. (I now realize she could have had a mullet and looked great.) I got my hair cut to look just like hers. It didn't quite look like I had imagined it. I went to some little salon in Chatsworth and pointed at her picture and said, "I want my hair like this." They cut it all right, though I didn't look like Michelle Pfeiffer when they were done. When I went in to read the second time, I think the chopped hairdo gave me a bit more of an offbeat look.

I was one of three girls who went to the network one morning to read with Kirk. During my audition it was immediately obvious that we read great together. That afternoon my dad got a phone call at his office from *TV Guide*, saying they wanted to schedule me at such and such a time that afternoon. My dad was confused.

"*TV Guide*? What are you talking about?"

The guy from *TV Guide* said, "Hasn't Business Affairs called you yet to book Tracey?"

They hadn't. *TV Guide* had broken the news. The guy was like, "Ummm, forget this phone call. Call us back after you talk to the network."

So that very afternoon I was at a photo shoot, having my picture taken with the other cast members for the fall *TV Guide* issue.

I had known Kirk for a long time. We had done a McDonald's commercial together when I was about twelve. He was just another fourteen-year-old kid when we started *Growing Pains*, not the teen heartthrob he would soon become.

I got home that night and I was like, *OK, I've gotten a series, what do I do with it?* Because at this point I had been thinking I would do more serious types of roles. I had learned a lot from Alan Parker on *Shoot the Moon*, and a sitcom hadn't been what I wanted to do. Missy had been shooting *Benson* for six years by this time. She loved it; it had been a great job for her. I still saw myself as a dramatic actress. As goofy and silly as I had been when I was a kid, that side grew less and less apparent as I got older. To be on a comedy series and told "you need to be bigger, broader, sillier..." was a switch for me after being told for so long that "less is more."

I sat home that night and watched the pilot of *Growing Pains* with my parents. Kirk and his mother Barbara had given it to us so we could see what this new show was all about. About halfway through I said, "Hmmm... I would actually watch this show. It's good." Up until that moment I didn't really know if it was any good or not. As a kid actress, I took work as it came and didn't really worry about a career strategy. But I got excited as I watched the pilot, realizing that this show might really be something fun. If you had told me that night that this new job would last for seven years, I never would have believed it.

Chapter Five

Home Away from Home

It only took me about a week to feel that I was a part of the *Growing Pains* group. I was a newcomer—the rest of the cast had all already worked together, and I was a bit nervous being the new kid on the block. But after a very short time I felt that I was part of a great new family.

It's always hard going into new situations. I always worry, *Will they like me? Will I fit in?* But my fears melted away quickly. Being a part of a long-running series is a phenomenal experience. The first couple years of *Growing Pains* were so exciting and thrilling, especially for a teenager. The premiere parties, the ABC Christmas party, photo shoots, gifts from the network... to be sixteen and have it all be so brand new and exciting made this an amazing time in my life.

I had spent the past six years watching my sister Missy on *Benson.* Sometimes I went to visit her and hang out on the set, but there I was just the sister. She got showered with so much great stuff. Of course it was superficial, but it was so fun. When I got *Growing Pains*, I sort of looked around and realized that this was my chance to get all the perks that come with being a part of a successful sitcom. I had never worked before a live audience. The whole experience was fresh and new.

When the weekends came I would actually be bummed out, because I couldn't wait to get back to work on Monday. Pure fun is what it was for the first couple of years. At the age of sixteen I had already been on two failed shows. I had done two series that hadn't gone: *Shirley* when I was a kid and *Goodnight Beantown* starring Bill Bixby when I was fourteen. (Incidentally, *Goodnight Beantown* was shot on the same lot, Warners Ranch, and on the very same stage where I wound up shooting *Growing Pains* for seven years.)

Growing Pains was successful with the public from the start, though not a blockbuster breakaway hit. The reviews were pretty bad in the beginning, but that didn't affect me too much. I had long ago learned that good reviews didn't mean that people watched the show in question. The show was never a critical darling like *Family Ties* or *Cosby*. A show is either in the critically acclaimed category, with Emmy nominations and so on, or it's not. *Growing Pains* was not—though we did get an Emmy nomination for Best Lighting one year—George Dibie—and won.

Over the years Kirk and I had often been paired together as brother and sister in commercials and movies because we looked so much alike as kids. I also knew his mother Barbara and his whole family quite well, which gave me some comfort going into the new show.

Joanna Kerns was immediately wonderful to me. She was a beautiful, glamorous blond woman. It's funny for me to realize now that she was younger at that time than I am now. She was only 32 years old when she played my mom on the show, really almost too young in real life to play the mother of teenagers. We were close right from the start. Alan Thicke was great too. The wonderful thing about Alan is his great sense of humility. He was always willing to laugh at himself. He had a little bit of almost dorkiness to him that was very endearing.

I looked at Jeremy as a pesky younger brother that I'd never had. At first I was like, *Who is this little boy farting next to me?* But soon I came to love him. He truly became the little brother I'd never had. There were so many parties and fun times and gatherings during those first few years. We'd get together on holidays, birthdays, everything. It sounds like a cliché, but our group was truly a family. Joanna would host parties; my parents, as always, hosted parties. On Halloween we'd have elaborate costume parties for the cast and crew. We were a very close group.

Kirk, Jeremy, and I shared a tutor for the first year of the show. After that one season, our tutor retired from teaching altogether. I never found out all the details of the situation, but we were told that she had left the show, quit teaching, and in fact would never teach again after one year of dealing with the three of us. By the first month of the second season it became apparent that Jeremy needed his own teacher. He was in a completely different age bracket than Kirk and I. So Kirk and I got our own teacher, Ben Freedman, who stayed with us for the rest of our time on the show. He was a kind teacher who had been married for about fifty years. He was a gentle older man, very mellow, which is just what you need when you're a kid working on a show. Jeremy got his own teacher, Milly Sacks, who had been my teacher a few times. She, too, was great. These schooling arrangements stayed in place until the end.

Kirk's popularity was immediate and immense. The creator of *Growing Pains* based a great deal of the show on his own life experiences. The character of Mike Seaver, played by Kirk, was very near and dear to the creator's heart. Six months into *Growing Pains,* there was a switch in the producers. The original creators parted ways with the show, and a new crew took over. After the show's creator left, the new writers fleshed out the other characters a bit more.

My character, Carol Seaver, was written in a very clichéd way, as the nerdy bookworm girl. As the show went on the writers eventually brought in many of my own characteristics and put them into Carol's character, particularly my naïvete and gullibility. All that stuff about boys and dating, that in real life I was insecure and shy about, they brought into Carol's character. Carol was the polar opposite of me in terms of academic achievement. She was a brain, and I wasn't. I struggled through school, like Mike Seaver did.

Carol eventually became a very well-rounded character. She dated, was popular with her peers, and even became homecoming queen. She really had it all toward the end. From starting out as a typical TV nerd I really got to expand and play a great character. It was a terrific job— one I'm very proud of, in spite of the eighties hair.

For four years it was the most wonderful job imaginable. I worked from August through March and took summers off. That was my time to play and go with my family on vacation. We were still living way out in Chatsworth, 25 miles outside of Los Angeles proper, far removed from Burbank and Hollywood. I grew up in a very protected environment, very far from L.A. as people imagine it. The Chatsworth house had a paddle tennis court, a pool, a gazebo... it was like our own private park. I shopped at malls, played with my sisters, and had a very regular, idyllic existence when I wasn't working.

I've always said that my sister Missy was like my best friend who got to spend the night with me every night. I didn't have many friends in high school—really any— and I didn't need them or miss them. Homework and tests and grades continued to be the bane of my existence. By the time I was a junior in high school it had reached the point where my parents would study with me at night. They could see that I was putting in the hours and doing all the work, but continued to do poorly on exams.

They took me to an educational psychologist for a month-long series of tests. The diagnosis: ADD (attention deficit disorder). Once again, this was way before the ADD label was thrown around like it is today and used for everybody. It was a relief to get this diagnosis; I felt like it proved I wasn't dumb, that there was finally a real reason why I couldn't do well at school—certain parts of my brain just didn't function the same as other parts. I wasn't stupid. My parents, too, were relieved to get to the root cause of my poor school performance. I think they felt a little bad about all the years they had been so hard on me about my grades, not realizing it had been out of my control. I had probably been overcompensating for my condition for years.

In my senior year I was allowed extra time to take my tests, and I was excused from classes such as calculus, in which I would clearly be in over my head. I attended an excellent Catholic college preparatory school, Chaminade High School in Chatsworth, which had very high academic standards and was geared to getting students into the best colleges in the country. I was required to take a number of tough college prep courses to graduate. Because of my ADD the school relaxed my requirements a bit (which they, along with most other schools, do these days as a matter of course for students with ADD or dyslexia). I was very glad, because there was no way I could have passed, much less gotten good grades.

Kirk escorted me to my senior prom. I was never so popular. We went as friends, there was nothing romantic about it. I had never dated, never had a boyfriend. In fact, I had my first kiss on TV! Joanna and Alan played a joke on me on that show where Carol Seaver got her first kiss. My dad pretended to storm onto the set and yelled "Hey! What are you doing to my daughter?" right in the middle of my scene. It was very funny, but just so mortifying to a sixteen-year-old girl. I wanted to crawl into a hole and die. I was certainly living out my "growing pains" on camera.

Even after high school I never did much dating. I was painfully shy around boys. As glamorous as being on *Growing Pains* might appear—and parts of it were—for the most part I had a very ordinary life. I never made the "party rounds." There were lots of teen clubs at the time that many young actors frequented, but I never did. I just didn't care about the whole premiere, go-out-and-be-seen-and-photographed circuit. When I went home I was part of a big, very close family. With the arrival of baby Jessie, I now had three sisters to play with and parents I loved. It was a wonderful, safe family circle, and I was in no hurry to leave it.

And at work we all got along tremendously well. The scripts were well-written, the show was funny and very popular in the ratings. Life was great, but I always had small moments of insecurity. I was very much in the public eye, and I had started out as a nerdy character.

On one hand I felt very "cool" to be on a show, but on the other hand never felt like the cool one. I worried that I wasn't pretty enough, all that sort of stuff. I never was a super-confident girl. I had all the normal, average teenage insecurities. But for the time being everything was going so smoothly that they very rarely came to the surface.

Chapter Six

"Not Eating" Days

After I graduated from high school I got to be on the set alone, without a teacher, which was a lot of fun. When you're a kid on a set you never get a break. If you're not working, you're getting tutored. When you're an adult you can go into your dressing room and watch TV and hang out a little bit. I felt grown-up and independent. I was also thrilled to have the torture of school behind me. If I never took another test in my entire life I would be a very happy girl.

College wasn't in the cards for me. I had found my life's work at the age of four and was delighted to be able to work full-time. Missy wound up heading east to go to college at Georgetown the next year, and I enjoyed visiting her: staying in the dorms, hanging out and soaking up the college scene. I would have liked the social aspects of college, but I was very relieved to be done with school. I was also locked into a successful series at the peak of its popularity. At the time it was out of the question that I would even consider leaving, for college or anything else. My dad says I went to the college of Warner Bros. I loved my job and was happy to be free of academic pressure.

My parents had been trying hard for another baby. My mom had had such a hard time conceiving Jessie, and had recently suffered through a miscarriage. My dad was firm: "This time we're going to adopt." Adopting was something they had always wanted to do, and they set about the process.

As the parents of four girls, at first they had hoped for a boy. While the whole family was taking a trip to Big Bear, they missed the call saying a baby boy had suddenly become available for adoption. This was before the days of cell phones. They missed that phone call by an hour at the most. By the time they got the message, it was too late. He had a new home. My mom was devastated and told my dad, "I don't care about the sex anymore. I want the next baby who comes along, boy or girl."

My parents were in the delivery room when my sister Cassie was born. It was an open adoption and they became friendly with her mother during her pregnancy.

Cassie has had an ongoing relationship with her—my parents made sure that Cassie knew her biological mother had wanted her and loved her enough to give her to people who could give her a great life. From the time she was very small, people would ask my parents, "Are you going to tell her she's adopted?" My mom would look at them like they were nuts. Cassie is half-Mexican, and in our blond family she would have realized fairly quickly that she looked very different. So she always knew she was adopted, especially wanted, and cherished.

The spring that I turned nineteen I went to Kansas City to perform in a play called *I Ought To Be In Pictures*. *Growing Pains* was on hiatus. I was living away from home for the first time and I put on some pounds. It was my version of the dreaded "Freshman 15." I was eating late at night after performances. I was far from home and my regular schedule, and there was no one to cook for me. I was eating whatever crap I wanted, and going out to dinner every night after the show. Just your regular late-teenager bad eating habits, like everyone has. It was fun, but I paid for it.

When I got back to work for the new season of *Growing Pains* I was quite aware that I had put on weight. But at first I wasn't really bothered by it. I just felt like, *Hey, it's not a big deal. I'm having fun, things are good. It'll come off.* Over the years there had been the occasional joke about my weight on the show in the context of brotherly teasing. But I suddenly could not escape them—it felt like every other page of my weekly script contained a fat joke. Naturally this was very upsetting to me. When I brought it up, the producers assured me that it was just brother/sister banter. I didn't have a brother, so I couldn't be expected to be familiar with that kind of teasing. They also pointed out that if it were really true, they wouldn't say it. Wanting to believe, I would say, "Well, OK," and try to put it out of my mind.

But after they reassured me, my father would inevitably get a phone call at his office in his official capacity as my agent. The producers would say flat out, "Tracey really needs to lose some weight." It put my dad in a very awkward position—he would have to come to me and say, "Tracey, I got a call from the producers...." That was all he ever needed to say. We both knew exactly what they were calling about. The conflicting messages I got were very disturbing.

In hindsight, it's obvious to me that the weight would have come off on its own. It would have leveled itself out—I had never had a weight problem before. I want to be perfectly clear that being told to lose weight for my job was not the reason I developed anorexia ner-

Growing Pains
cast and crew
– 1986

The Gold Girls – 1988

Doing "I Ought To
Be In Pictures"
my 'freshman 15'

Jessie & Cassie

vosa. Someone who was not predisposed to this disease would have been able to laugh the jokes off, or simply lose the excess weight and keep going. I can't, and don't, put the blame on other people, because truthfully it's an addiction or weakness like any other—I have to take responsibility for it. And I do.

That being said, the pressure certainly didn't help. My self-esteem was shot. I felt so ugly. I was the fat, ugly little sister. If you happen to catch *Growing Pains* in reruns you'll see episodes where I look heavy. It's very hard for me to watch. I was a little pudgy, there's no denying it. But the responsibility an actress has to look a certain way is different for a teenager than it is for an adult woman. My job in that role was not to be a sex symbol—I was playing a teenage girl.

I was feeling so self-conscious about the jokes and my weight that I couldn't stand it anymore. Every week I would get the script and pray that it wouldn't contain any fat jokes. There were so many, and each one filled me with such shame and embarrassment. I decided it was time to go on a diet and lose the weight. My parents, to their credit, didn't want me to go on some crazy haphazard diet. Given my history with anorexia, they were worried, and wanted me to go to a medical doctor where I would be professionally supervised. *Let's send her to a good doctor and do this properly*, was their thought. The night before I went to the doctor for my initial visit, I knew I was going to get weighed and put on a strict diet, so I asked my mom to make pasta carbonara for dinner. It was my favorite.

My mom has always been an amazing cook, and the kitchen was always the center of our home. Mom is of Czechoslovakian descent, and made the most incredible fattening treats, especially at holiday times: pirogis, halushkis, all kinds of great stuff. She made wonderful meals for the family the whole time I was growing up. I knew I'd better get one last good meal in—this is how normal my eating habits were at that time. I had my big hurrah farewell dinner. It was delicious.

The doctor I went to see was an endocrinologist. He had just published a new diet book and obviously wanted me to try his new plan. Knowing full well that I'd had a bout with anorexia at age 12, he told me, "You can go on a 1,000-calorie-a-day diet or a 500-calorie-a-day diet. On the 500-calorie-a-day diet you'll lose weight in half the time." At this point I was more than ready to do whatever it took. All I wanted to do was get rid of the extra pounds I was carrying around.

When I had finally decided to see a doctor, I was hoping in the back of my mind that I might have a thyroid problem, or some other minor medical condition of that nature. I thought it was very possible that maybe all I needed was a little medication. I had never had a weight problem before; the extra pounds were a very recent addition. I was secretly kind of thinking that I might be prescribed a magic pill and presto, I'd lose the weight.

But no, he tested me, and there was nothing wrong with my thyroid. It was junk food eating, plain and simple, that had made me gain the weight. There was no magic pill. The doctor said, "You should definitely get on this diet." I was calculating in my head, *In a month I could lose this many pounds. I know it'll be hard for the time I have to do it but then this will be over and I'll be back to my regular self...*

I was up on the scale being weighed as the doctor was talking to me, looking at that horrible marker on that horrible number. And of all the outfits to wear... on that particular day I had on orange shorts. With black socks, no less. I felt terribly exposed and ashamed. My self-esteem was so low... I couldn't stand to look the way I did for another minute. I felt so fat and ugly. *That's it, I want this over with. Now,* I thought and picked the 500-calorie a day diet. Fast and simple.

My mind was made up. I stuck to the plan and obvious-ly lost weight fast. I was a model patient. My parents were very supportive during this time because when the producers were unhappy with my weight it put my dad in a really uncomfortable position. Getting those phone calls was hard on him, too. Strictly from an agent's standpoint, as a working actress I did need to lose some weight. My parents were very aware of the pitfalls of dieting but were reassured because after all, I was under a doctor's care. I was on the diet from October to Christmastime of 1988. Right when I started that diet is when I bought the official doctor's medical scale that I would forever after weigh myself on—the kind you stand on and move the ticker back and forth so it records your *exact* weight.

At the family home in Chatsworth we all ate our meals together, and my mom, as always, cooked a great dinner for everyone each night. My new diet was briefly the sub-ject of everyone's interest. My parents went out of their way to encourage me and help me stick to my new eat-ing plan. During this time it was specifically known that I had to eat very particular foods. Usually I ran out and grabbed a take-out salad and ate it while everyone else ate their regular dinner. It was no big deal, because the diet started out as a good thing. Very soon I was looking better and eating in a healthier manner, so whatever plan I was following was OK with my parents.

It took only a couple of months to get down to my ideal weight—a loss of 20 pounds. I'd always had a fast metabolism so I achieved the weight loss fairly quickly and easily. I maintained this new, close-to-perfect weight for about a year. It might have fluctuated a bit up and down—sometimes a couple of pounds more, sometimes a couple of pounds less—but I was basically stable at an ideal weight for me.

In March my family made a huge move, this time to a grand new house in Valley Village. I was out of high school and anxious for some independence—my little bedroom in the family house wasn't doing it for me anymore. But the previous summer Rebecca Schaeffer from the popular show *My Sister Sam* had been murdered by a deranged fan. Our stages had been next door to each other so I saw her frequently. We were very close in age—she was just a bit older than me—and I had always looked up to her as such a beautiful girl. In the aftermath of her murder, and the resulting media uproar about celebrity stalking, it became very clear how careful actresses needed to be with their personal safety. I certainly wasn't ready to move to my own apartment or house and live alone.

So my parents had searched for a new home with a guest-house on the property for me. The new house was on a one-acre plot and had an old pool house that would suit my needs. I put a lot of money and effort into renovating the decrepit structure, where I lived alone. My first place! It was the perfect compromise because I had my independence and my own place, but I still felt safe and was near my family—across the pool, to be exact.

When you walked into my cottage there was a huge fireplace and a little kitchen area with a dining table. The house had a bedroom and a pink bathroom with a sunken tub and custom tile work. There were French doors with light wood and hand-painted tiles throughout. It had pink carpet and shelves for my doll collection—I've been collecting dolls since I was nine years old. It was the perfect little dream cottage for me, the reflection of my personality and everything I loved. I was thrilled with how I had transformed such a nasty old pool house into a beautiful little dollhouse. Even as much as I loved my new home, I continued to spend the majority of my time at the main house with my family. I usually went home to my little house only to sleep.

For probably close to a year after completing my diet I continued to eat in a very healthy way. But very gradually I started to slide into a new plan, one that consisted of "eating days" and "not-eating days." The best way to describe this plan was that I would not eat a single bite of food all week from Monday through Thursday—nothing.

I would drink Diet Coke and tea, and on the weekends I would binge-eat whatever I wanted on Friday, Saturday and Sunday. Monday through Thursday were the non-eating days. Of course it didn't start out quite this drastically, but very soon that was the pattern I fell into.

When I look back and try to trace the progression from following a strict diet, losing weight, eating pretty healthily and maintaining a good weight, to eating days/not-eating days, I think what happened is that I felt so restricted in what I could and couldn't eat after that diet that I said to myself: *There have to be some days where I can just indulge myself and eat whatever I want.* So I allowed myself those days, but to counteract them I set up my schedule as eating days/not-eating days. It was all or nothing—I could see no in-between. Gradually it began to take over my whole life. I made no secret of what I was doing, and at first my parents were accepting of this new plan.

As the months passed I really honed and refined the pattern of my days—eating on some, not eating on most. My family was accustomed to me eating differently than the rest of them, and I was maintaining a good weight, so no one was alarmed at this point. If I said it was a not-eating day, everyone just said OK and didn't think too much about it. It was easy to stick to my schedule because I didn't have much of a social life anyway. It was: go to work, come home, watch a little TV, daydream about food and my weight, and go to bed.

While I was doing this radical eating plan, the first couple days always felt good. It was kind of cleansing and refreshing on the first day or two that I didn't eat, like going on a juice fast or something. Believe me, on "eating days" I consumed enough junk food to feed a small nation. But by the end of the week I would definitely get light-headed and dizzy and start to feel tired... I was starving. I would dream about food. I'd be thinking the whole time *I can't wait until Friday. . . I can't wait until Friday. . . I want to eat so badly. . .* I lived for weekends, when I could eat whatever I pleased.

I planned my whole week around those few days I would allow myself to eat. On Fridays I would eat pizza, chips, candy... everything my heart desired. I kept my doctor's scale over at my parents' house, and at this point I wasn't weighing myself every day. I only weighed myself once a week, on Fridays. If I hadn't gained any weight it was my entrée to decadence—my weekend binge where I could eat whatever I wanted. When Monday came I would start another week of *no eating*. The problem with this plan was that by the end of the week I was a walking zombie. I was hungry, tired and obsessed with food. It got to the point where I read cookbooks just for fun. I needed to look at pictures of food to satiate myself, and plan what I would eat on the weekends. It was a miserable existence I was creating.

At this time I don't think people on the set of *Growing Pains* noticed anything was wrong. Nobody took issue with this kind of odd eating behavior, because I kept it well hidden. We all usually went our own ways for lunch, so I never had to explain what I was doing. Although at home, after a while my dad started to get pissed off—and concerned—about my eating habits.

"Who doesn't eat all week, I don't understand this, Tracey!"

And my mom would be like, "It's OK, Harry, she eats fine on the weekend. Let her be."

The process was becoming very regimented and strict in my mind. Once when I was sick with a really bad cold my mom said, "Here, you need to take some cough syrup."

I said "Absolutely not. I am not taking cough syrup."

When she asked why I said, "Because today's a not-eating day."

She said, "Tracey, there are no calories in cough syrup!"

And I told her, "It doesn't matter, because I'm not having it." And I didn't.

This incident really got my mom's attention. She said to me, "This is ridiculous. This craziness *has* to stop."

But it didn't.

Chapter Seven

Roby – True Love

I met Roby, my first boyfriend, first love, and the man I would eventually marry, on the set of *Growing Pains*. He was working as a technical consultant/production assistant on the set of *Blind Faith*, an NBC miniseries based on Joe McGinniss's true-crime book about a seemingly picture-perfect wealthy New Jersey family. The wife was brutally murdered, and though her husband was, on the surface, a loving family man, it eventually became clear that he had a sordid secret life and had killed the mother of his children for her $2 million-dollar life insurance policy. Joanna Kerns portrayed Maria, the beautiful, vivacious wife and loving mother of three boys: Roby, Chris and John. Maria was Roby's mother.

I remembered my father reading the new hardcover while we were on vacation in Hawaii the previous summer. My sister Brandy had played one of the little girls who was murdered in a movie based on another one of Joe McGinniss's books, *Fatal Vision. Blind Faith,* his latest, had been highly anticipated, and my dad was anxious to read it. It was a huge bestseller—everyone was reading it. My dad related the whole story to the rest of us as we lounged on the beach. A few months later, Joanna had done everything she could to be allowed to take the role of Maria in the movie. It was rare back then for a series to allow actors time off to do other projects. The *Growing Pains* producers were swayed in part by the fact that Roby was so adamant that Joanna was the only woman who should play this role. She was his only choice.

Roby had learned the hard way how difficult it is to maintain control over your own story once it becomes a part of the public record. He had taken a job on the production staff of the movie to protect his mother's memory and make sure she was portrayed accurately. Everything turned out well. Joanna had been given the time off to do the movie of the week and play his mother, just as he had wished.

Joanna was crazy about Roby, too, thought he was just a great guy. She told me, "I'd better introduce him to somebody his own age before I take him for myself!" He was twenty-four years old. I was a *very* young twenty.

The greatest gift
I ever got – Roby
and Diet Coke!
December 1989

My world is rocked
– April 1990

Young Love –
Las Vegas June 1990

Romeo and Juliet
– Halloween 1991

She brought him to the set for the taping of the show one night. I was in the Smith House, a run-down old house on the Warner Ranch where tables were set up for dinner each evening. I wasn't really eating dinner at this point, but I went in to socialize. I was in a bathrobe and wearing glasses because Carol Seaver was sick in that night's episode. Not a very glamorous way to meet your future husband. Joanna brought Roby over and introduced him to everyone at the table. He sat down and said hi to me. When he headed over to the dessert table he politely asked, "Can I get you a cookie?" Of course I declined, but I was immediately smitten.

He was so tall, with blond hair and blue eyes, and just so manly looking, handsome... you name it. I was a little bit intimidated. This was not a boy—this was a man. I was a little disappointed because he didn't even stay for the whole taping; he left early to drive some friends to the airport. I had an immediate crush, but I wasn't about to say anything to anybody, because I would have been teased mercilessly. If I had mentioned Roby it would have been the running joke on the set for at least a week. Plus, I was very shy around the opposite sex. I wouldn't have said anything, but Joanna did. She started gently teasing me, saying things like, "Somebody's been talking about you!" and telling me that he would be coming back soon to visit.

I was thrilled when he came to the set again and made it very clear that he wanted to get to know me. I'm glad he did, because I was so shy, still a kid in so many ways, I would have let him slide right by if he hadn't made a big effort. He really pursued me, and I loved it. He was older, really good-looking—he had been a lifeguard on the Jersey shore for eight years, Speedo and all. He *wasn't* an actor. I had been around actors all my life and the idea of dating them didn't interest me. I was always afraid of going out with someone whose jeans were smaller than mine! Roby was a whole different kind of guy—meeting him and having him pursue me was absolutely life-changing.

Just a week after meeting him he had to go back east for Christmas. What do you give someone you've only known a week but are extremely interested in? Well Roby, the clever and romantic guy he is is, filled up the back of his truck with 12 cases of Diet Coke and a dozen pink roses and delivered them to me. He had quickly noticed that I was never without it and wanted to bring me something I would like. I was overjoyed by the present—I do love my Diet Coke—but even happier that he made such an effort to please me and had noticed the details. I was walking on a cloud.

At the time I met him I didn't consider myself sick—nobody did. My eating days/not-eating days were very well established, but anorexia hadn't yet overtaken my life. I didn't know enough to think that my eating patterns were weird or unhealthy. I continued to be pretty up front about what I did. I thought, and I would tell people if they asked, *This is what I do. This is how I maintain my weight.* I wasn't losing weight at this point; I was just holding steady, and still looked healthy and good.

After a few dates Roby took me out for a nice dinner. It was a not-eating day so naturally I didn't eat a single bite. Roby ate his meal while I drank a Diet Coke. He was kind of freaked out by this behavior. He said flat out, "What do you mean... you have *not-eating* days?" He's a big guy, six-foot-four to be exact, from New Jersey; he likes his food. For the life of him he could not understand not-eating days.

I was obsessed with him. I adored him so much, and I was afraid that my strange habits would interfere with the relationship that was blooming and keep us from going out on dinner dates and other normal couple kinds of activities. I remember thinking, *I've got to find a new plan here, because this guy's not going to go for this.*

I had to eat on the nights I saw Roby—he insisted on it. So I ate a light meal on the days I was with him, and otherwise tried to readjust and shuffle my eating days and not-eating days. I was able to stick with this for a while. I was doing my best to keep the peace—that is, keep everyone off my back. I wanted to maintain control over my eating while convincing everyone that I was perfectly OK. In the back of my mind I always felt I could stay in control if I didn't eat *at all*. But if I ate anything at all I worried constantly—*did I just eat too much?*

My weight started to drop—very, very gradually at first. Roby and I continued to date, and we grew closer and closer, spending more and more time together. I always say that Roby and I fell instantly in love—there was no in-between. He rocked my world.

I would guess that in the first year Roby and I were together, I probably lost five pounds. Some of this had to do with the fact that this was the first time I was sexually active, and I had the usual concerns about my body being seen in its entirety. It was important to me to be perfect, as it is for so many girls. I was so enraptured in my perfect love affair and romance... I wanted Roby to think I was beautiful. He was four years older than I was, and he'd had plenty of girlfriends in his life. Roby loved me and did everything he could to show it, but I felt insecure thinking of all the girls he'd known before me. The internal pressure in me to be perfect intensified.

Dating and falling in love is so much about going out together and eating and enjoying good food. It's really such a big part of what life is all about. The year I started dating Roby was the first year I was really living a new, more independent kind of life. Before that, I hadn't gone out too much. I had worked and spent time with my family. And quite frankly, I hadn't much cared if my eating habits irritated my parents. They were my parents, after all: I knew they would love me no matter what. If they were annoyed or concerned, I knew I could handle it. But when Roby questioned my behavior, I knew I had to make some adjustments fast. The last thing I wanted was for him to wonder, *What is wrong with this girl I'm dating? I can't handle a girl who won't eat. This is too much to deal with—it's not worth it. She's not worth it.* I tortured myself, imagining that he might have these thoughts.

I still looked fine. After Roby and I had been dating for about six months I played a cheerleader in an after-school special directed by Tom Skerritt and looked great in it, though I only *felt* great on my eating days. The shuffling of eating/not-eating days was taking up a lot of time and effort.

So I came up with a new idea. It was that I would try a different, more normal eating pattern. My journal entry from that time spells it out this way: *I will eat one meal a day*

*(a light meal) and leave two days—Friday and Saturday—
for eating days—without my Fritos. I am so nervous this
won't work. If I gain an ounce I'll be so upset!*

(Please, let me just state here that at this moment, as
I write this book, I can't even relate to the girl who
wrote those scared words.)

My other strange food habits came into play around this
time too. Today everybody talks about carbohydrates as
such a big no-no. For the record, carbs were all I ever
ate! Pasta, in particular. I wouldn't prepare the food I
ate myself—I had a weird thing about doing that. I
guess because I had started my diet eating a lot of
restaurant food, it's what made me feel safe. Cook for
other people, yes—I loved doing that. Most anorexics
do. I would cook the most fattening food and not eat it.
But I'd make treats for Roby and expect him to eat
them, which of course he always did.

For myself, I only ate from my "safe" restaurants. I would
only eat lunch at Chin-Chin and dinner at California Pizza
Kitchen. I knew if I ate set meals each day I could maintain my weight. For four straight years—well into my
recovery—I ordered the same dinner each night: tomato
basil angel hair pasta. And bagels. For a long time I ate
a bagel for lunch. All carbs!

I always say I was a lazy anorexic. I hate exercise. I hate gyms. I hate to sweat. I'm a naturally active and high-energy person. And having New York blood in me, I love to walk. At lunchtime I took walks instead of having a meal. I would go shopping instead of having lunch. That's what I did while everyone else ate—I shopped.

Hunger comes in waves, and I trained myself to work through my hunger. When I was really hungry and feeling faint, if I rode it out all of a sudden I'd be all right again—not hungry. Then a couple hours later I'd get really hungry again, but I'd stick it out some more. I could bide my time until dinner.

I started using the word 'anorexia' in my journals, admitting to myself that I had once again fallen into it. My parents, Roby and I all agreed that I needed to see someone about eating issues, so I started to see a psychiatrist regularly. We all wanted to nip anorexia in the bud again, just as I had when I was twelve.

* * *

By the beginning of 1991 I was starving myself and throwing up, and I couldn't hide it any longer. My psychiatrist was doing me more harm than good. I had convinced him that I needed a prescription diuretic—for my PMS, I told him. To help you understand how destructive my behavior was, when I would arrive for each therapy session, I would purge beforehand in his bathroom. I was going through the motions with no intention of really focusing on my problem.

I couldn't stop my downward spiral. Roby and my family were very concerned about me. Roby tried to get me into an eating disorders program that was going on in a hospital right down the street from his apartment. He took me there and we spoke to someone, but I was not ready to admit how serious my problem really was. I thought I could handle it on my own. I always say how important it is to be aggressive in catching this problem early. I was slowly crossing over the line.

The truth is I've always been a bit weird about food. I love some things, hate some things, and could eat certain things over and over again and never get sick of them. Even as a kid, my eating habits tended to be monotonous. For years I had tuna melts every time my family ate in a restaurant, no matter how nice it was. I would order my tuna melt well done, and if it wasn't cooked just right I'd send it back. Way before I ever had anorexia, I had rigid food habits. My parents would urge me to try something new, but I'd always just want my tuna melt. I still ate the same things over and over now that I was older. I was never big on variety.

That summer Roby and I went to Mexico. We were sitting in a restaurant and I scanned the menu. I looked up and said to the waiter, "Do you have anything else besides Mexican food here?" I was serious. Despite my growing weirdness with food, we still had fun. It was one of the last carefree vacations we would have for quite some time.

Later that summer of 1991 I actually entered my first eating disorder program. Therapy alone clearly wasn't doing the trick; it was time for something more. I had lost a great deal of weight; I was visibly much too thin. The show was on hiatus. On July 2nd I started as an outpatient at Northridge Hospital Eating Disorder Unit for Adolescents. At this point my goal was to start eating three meals a day again. I wasn't doing eating/not-eating days or weekend eating whatever I wanted anymore. I had progressed to a very severe restriction on what I could and could not eat. I was losing weight rapidly because I was throwing up what little I did eat.

Northridge Hospital is where I met a lot of really sick girls. There were a number of "cutters" there—girls who cut themselves and mutilated their bodies. The girls who cut themselves were mostly bulimic—there seemed to be a connection between the two diseases. I didn't quite get it... I've never been a big fan of blood or pain, myself.

My Family
– 1991

Soooo sick –
even in Hawaii

A living
nightmare
– in spite
of the smile

I befriended a girl who was very seriously anorexic. Our friendship was rooted in our illness, and it was very unhealthy. This girl unwittingly taught me things I didn't know. I wasn't particularly concerned about fat grams and so on. She's the one who taught me to read the labels on the food packages and see how many grams of fat were in everything. This was in the very early 90s—it was just becoming a normal thing to read labels and scrutinize what was in the food you bought at the market.

The whole experience taught me that a group situation can be very detrimental for people with eating disorders. I knew I never wanted to seek help in a group situation again, because it devolved into this sick game of "Who's the best anorexic? Who's the sickest? Who are the doctors most worried about?" I started to question why I was even there, because I clearly wasn't the skinniest.

I went every day from 10:00 in the morning until 3:00 in the afternoon. They served lunch there, and they watched to make sure you ate the meal they prepared. If you didn't they had a can of Ensure waiting for you. Ensure is a liquid supplement with millions of calories. They used it as a threat: "If you don't eat your lunch, you're getting Ensure." They had some art therapy, and some group therapy, none of it particularly effective. It all felt very useless to me. Drawing and coloring so they could interpret my feelings? To this day I'm not really sure it's all that helpful.

During treatment I continued to see my regular psychiatrist, who was still prescribing me my diuretic. I was always able to charm doctors and divert the subject to get what I wanted. When you're anorexic or bulimic it's very common to become addicted to laxatives and diuretics—both of which I abused during this time. Real glamorous, huh?

At the end of the six-week program I had actually lost a few pounds. That isn't much, but when you're trying to *gain* weight... The outpatient program was a huge turning point for me. In those six weeks I became quite an expert anorexic. I learned plenty of new tricks. I wanted to become the "best anorexic," and I wasn't. To be the sickest was what I secretly desired.

I left the program knowing I had learned too much, scared of what I knew. Everyone wanted me to see a nutritionist—I could have written my own nutrition book. I had practically memorized every calorie counter known to man. My days were ruled by what I ate. I was obsessed with what I could or could not have. I read cookbooks incessantly. My mood and outlook were ruled by food and weight. I did not feel good unless the scale showed the number I wanted to see. If the "right" number popped up, a lower number would immediately become my next goal. I could never really enjoy myself or relax, even for a minute. I always had something new to attain and obsess about. My menstrual cycle disappeared, but I was so young that the thought of ruining my reproductive organs didn't scare me. It only reassured me that I was achieving my goal. Everyone noticed my drastic weight loss, which served as validation to keep going. I had no idea what a dangerous game I was playing. I thought I was finally in control and could stop before it took control of me. How little I knew.

Chapter Eight

Losing the Game

I was entering what would turn out to be the last season of *Growing Pains,* though we didn't know it at the time. Going back for a seventh season was difficult in several ways. I was really unhappy toward the end of the show's long run. The writing wasn't as sharp as it once was, and we had a new group of producers. As much as there was somewhat of a love/hate relationship between the cast and producers, the old producers certainly knew the characters. It was weird having these new people write for characters that we knew much better than they did. There were a lot of times I would read my dialogue and think, *My character wouldn't say that.*

The cast still loved each other, but there was some friction by this point. With Kirk in particular. He'd become a born-again Christian. He married Chelsea Noble, whom he met when she appeared in a recurring role as his love interest on *Growing Pains.* They would go on to adopt four kids, and then have two more of their own. Kirk alienated a lot of people at this time. He had a lot of control. He was a very, very popular character and he wielded a lot of power. He refused to do anything that was the least bit racy or controversial. He wanted a cookie-cutter little Ozzie and Harriet-type show, and this was at a time when grittier programming like *Roseanne* was coming on the air to great acclaim.

His new religious views were out of step with the prevailing trends. What he wanted was not what the general viewing public wanted. When he got married on the hiatus he didn't invite anyone from the show. All he said when he got back was, "We just wanted our close friends and family." We were all shocked—we *were* family, and he never even told us. It was very hurtful for all of us.

Growing Pains had just run its course. When we came back for the last year I was feeling very stuck. I just hid out in my dressing room. It became my refuge. As we headed into the seventh season I was still maintaining my low-hundreds weight. When you're on TV you go in for a fitting every week. My costumer, the wonderful Judith Brewer Curtis, would come in each week with all the new clothes they had bought for that week's episode, measure me, and fit the clothes to me. As an actress, you spend a lot of time looking in a mirror. You have people staring at you deciding what looks good on you and what doesn't, and it all becomes a real critical thing.

I think it's become a noticeable trend in the last decade of most TV shows that because of all this intense focus you can see a marked difference in the weights of all the actresses from the pilot to the third season. Even actors aren't immune to the pressure. Take a look at any show… you'll see what I mean.

I was feeling very unhappy, unsettled, and work just wasn't the same. I spent all my time away from work in my relationship. It was very intense; I was very much caught up in my first love. Roby was everything to me. He was my rock.

Around Halloween my weight started to drop even more drastically. It had gotten to the point where I was throwing up all the time, and Roby and my parents had figured out what was going on. I couldn't hide it anymore. When someone would come and eat lunch with me, I would run into my private bathroom and throw it up as soon as they left. It became quite a regular cycle. My problem was that sometimes I was forced to have meals with other people who expected me to eat. I would eat just enough so they would think I was getting better, then throw it all up the second they were gone.

I only ate normal meals, never enough to make me feel overstuffed or nauseous.

Other people were starting to notice that something was very wrong...my friends, the people at work. It was during this seventh season that Roby got so frustrated that he came to my dressing room one day and literally nailed my bathroom door shut so I couldn't throw up. As upset as I was that he took my bathroom away from me, I was also relieved. It took the power away from me.

The bottom really fell out of my world during the long grind of the show that last year. I had always been friendly and on good terms with everyone, but by this point everyone was starting to separate and do their own things. I became very isolated sitting in my dressing room alone.

That week of Halloween, when I dropped below one hundred pounds, was critical. When you have anorexia and you drop to a new, lower weight, an even lower number immediately becomes the new ideal. I was very caught up in this dangerous game. Once I went under that all-important 100-pound mark I wasn't about to go back up. I didn't, in fact, come back up for two years; I only went progressively lower.

I went to so many programs before I got better. I went to a body image class that didn't help. A well-meaning friend suggested Overeaters Anonymous (OA). I went to some meetings. I got a sponsor and everything—she was a lifelong anorexic. It didn't stop my descent into full-blown anorexia. From the start of that season until the end of the year I probably dropped ten pounds. My situation was clearly reaching the critical stage. I didn't look like myself. But more importantly, I didn't act like myself. I was a walking zombie. My eyes were blank. You can see it on some episodes of *Growing Pains*. My persona was so markedly changed. I was in a fog, could barely concentrate, was wooden-looking and hollow-sounding. To this day I can't remember any of the storylines from that season. Someone told me there was a Leo who worked on the show that year? Leo who? Clearly I was not all there.

It was very obvious that something was terribly wrong, but no one would do anything. Everyone was concerned, and people were always asking me if I was OK. I would assure them I was fine, I was working on it.

Everything came to a head after Christmas break. Just before I left for the holidays the new producers called me in and said, "Look, we're concerned. You've lost a lot of weight and we're all worried. We need to be guaranteed that you will put some weight back on." It was one of the most ironic moments of my life. But I said, "Trust me, I'll rest on vacation and when I come back I'll have gained a little weight. Just trust me, guys." And I meant it—I thought I could gain a couple pounds to appease them.

While I was home on Christmas vacation I became very ill with bronchitis. It was really rainy that year and I was constantly cold and shivering. Roby and I went away to Florida for New Year's—I think Roby always thought that a change of scenery would be the magic trip that would make me better. I only got worse while we were away—the bronchitis never fully cleared up, and it rained the whole time in Florida, too. I came back home feeling like death and having lost even more weight.

The first day back at work they called a doctor to come and see me because of my "bronchitis." When I stood up to get my pulse taken it dropped so dramatically that they told me to go home and rest. I said, OK, fine. I was relieved. I was exhausted; I just wanted to go home and sleep and hide. At the moment I associated being sent home with my bout of bronchitis. I wasn't even thinking that this could be about anorexia or my weight.

When I got home it turned out that my dad had gotten a phone call from Warner Bros. They had told him that

I was uninsurable and they wanted me in a hospital. They told my dad that I couldn't go back on the show until I got help. They had found what they thought would be a great program for me. It was the eating disorders unit at Edgemont Hospital.

I was off the show. I had never missed a day of work since I was four years old. Everything I had learned about being the ultimate professional didn't matter anymore. I just didn't care.

* * *

I was so tired. Roby and my parents were all relieved that things had come to a head and I was finally going to get some help. It was out of their hands. The couple of hours before we left for the hospital, I was in Roby's safe apartment and he engulfed me in a huge hug that must have lasted for over an hour. I was so sad and scared. All my "fears" faded against the terrible *real* fear of checking into the hospital. Roby and my dad drove me to the hospital at night. I was crying when I got there and was checked in. I said my good-byes and they left. That first night I crawled into the strange little bed, pulled the covers over my head and tried to go to sleep.

I had come in there thinking I would have to stay for about a week, having no idea that it was a four-week program. Once I got in there and realized it would be more like a month, it completely shocked me. I wasn't terribly clear on what it would take to get out of there. It was all based on the 12-step program. I was so caffeine addicted—I had basically been living on Diet Coke (which to this day, I admittedly still love)—and they took me off it cold turkey. I had major caffeine withdrawal, and that alone can make someone really sick. At this point when I weighed under 100 pounds, taking me off caffeine was a jolt to my fragile system. I kept telling everyone *I need something, please... I need aspirin, something, anything, please, the pain is so bad...*And they would say they were sorry but they couldn't give me anything until they had the doctor's approval. And he could never be found.

I shared a room with a woman with bulimia. When I entered the hospital I wasn't eating a lot, but the things I was allowing myself to eat were forbidden to me in the hospital! That was incomprehensible to me. I would have eaten some pasta from California Pizza Kitchen if I wasn't in this horrible place. But they were serving such low-calorie food: tofu and diet everything. There weren't any choices. No one watched me to make sure I was eating. As much as I hated being monitored, I was even more scared by the reality that no one *was* watching me. What kind of place was this?

The staff had warned my parents: "This is tough love. You do not talk to her while she's being treated here. She got herself into this position and she'll have to get herself out." I was not allowed to talk to anyone. Yet right outside my "room" was a pay phone, which I used freely, without permission, much to the consternation of the other patients. I always wanted to say to them "Hey. No one's stopping you—go ahead and use the phone!" I knew it was wrong, but I couldn't help it. I got in trouble for it, but I didn't care. I *had* to talk to someone. I would call my parents' home and inevitably get seven-year-old Jessie, who had been told to hang up on me. Roby was the only one who took my calls. Never one to follow orders, God bless him.

It was a cold and scary place. And it didn't specialize in anorexia—the program was for overeaters, anorexics and bulimics. People weighing under 100 pounds were treated alongside others who weighed 400-plus. As I said, everyone's treatment was all based on the 12-step program, similar to the OA program I had been in prior to my hospitalization. They wanted you to go through all the steps. My plan was to get through every step in a week and get out: *I'm writing my first step down and I'm outta here as soon as possible.*

I was at rock bottom. I couldn't believe what my life had come to. On the first morning at 5:30, I had been awakened to attend an exercise class. Hello—*exercise*? What were they thinking? We had counseling, weigh-ins, and nutrition classes. I don't believe in nutrition classes for anorexics—it puts too much focus on food. They would show us plastic models of food portions so we could see how much was OK to have. I swear, if I saw one more piece of plastic food... And it always looked too small! Really, I think I ate more than those plastic portions! They were the *smallest* portions of food I had ever seen.

JOURNAL ENTRY/LETTER TO ROBY:

I'm sitting here in my bed right now but something tells me I should write. It's breakfast now but it's optional so I've opted not to eat. Please don't get mad but I just can't deal with going into the dining room right now. I'll eat my lunch though.

They woke me up to take my blood. The sun is just com-ing up now. I can see it out my window. My roommate's clock makes the most annoying tick-tock noise. You'd be going out of your mind. I slept with the blankets over my head to lessen the noise. Roby, this place is really scary. I can't believe it's only 6:30 a.m. and I'm already dressed and ready for my day. Roby, I don't know if this is the right place for me. Everyone is so much older than me. I feel so lonely, writing to you helps though.

Knowing some day you'll read this and understand what I'm feeling.

Now it's about 11:30 in the morning and I'm so sad and lonely. I want to come home. Nobody here is like me, I can't relate to anyone. I want you to be proud of me but I want out. How is anyone supposed to heal here? I don't know. I feel so much pressure inside myself. I don't know how to explain it. I'm losing my mind here. I feel totally out of touch with reality. There's a whole world going on outside of here. Roby, how did I ever get myself into this mess? How can I get out of it? I need to see you now. Right now.

My survival instincts really kicked into gear; I knew that I had to get out. I started asking around to other patients and the staff, and learned you could sign yourself out. I went in to talk with some of the doctors and administrators and I said to them, "I don't think this is working for me; I think I need to leave." They said, "We advise you not to." I said: "I can't stand it here; this doesn't feel right to me." They said, "We're telling you if you leave this place you will die." And I said, "Well I'd rather die on the outside than die in here. I prefer to die at home." And so I made the choice to leave. I hated it so much that it scared me more to be in there than to think I might die.

So I left against medical advice. I lugged my overstuffed suitcases through the hospital and called a cab to go home. I had brought three huge bags filled with all my best clothes with me. And the whole time everyone around me was in sweatpants. The other patients barely even got dressed, and there I was, up every morning doing my hair and putting on makeup. I had to re-pack my three huge suitcases, which I had barely made a dent in. I had lasted an entire three days.

I couldn't get ahold of anybody on the phone to tell them of this huge decision. Walking out of that hospital was the most outwardly rebellious act of my life. I had always been a good girl, a real "pleaser," but something in me knew that this was not the right thing for me. The hospital was hurting me, not helping. I had no choice but to leave. *I'm going to prove you all wrong*, I thought as I left. I got into a cab and went home, not knowing how I would be received when I got there. My mom saw the cab pull up outside our house and gave me a big hug when I walked through the door.

I think my parents had been nervous about the hospital's tough love approach, but they'd put all their faith in people who "knew better." Everyone was scared. What would we do now? My parents were adamant. They agreed that the hospital might not have been the right place for me, but they sat me down and told me I had to make a commitment to doing something else.

JOURNAL ENTRY – WEEK OF JANUARY 13TH:
This is the toughest week I've ever gone through. 3 days in that place was enough to never want to go through anything like that again. For the first time in my life I don't care what anyone else thinks; **I know I only have myself.** *This week has been like a bad dream. Is this my life? I know I'm going to see it in all the magazines. That is so maddening. I feel so much pressure. I have no choice but to get help and get better. When will I go back to work? How will I get better? Who can help me?*

Of course I felt bad because I had to call the head of Warner Bros. and tell him that I'd left the hospital against medical advice but I planned to get help. They told me that they were choosing to believe that I meant what I said about trying to get better, and they would keep an eye on me and see how I was doing.

Incredibly, one week to the day after I had lain in my hospital bed suffering from a caffeine-withdrawal migraine, I went to the movies in the middle of the day. It was a weekday afternoon, and there was my doctor from Edgemont Hospital walking into the theater. It must have been his regular schedule. I wanted to go up to him and say, "Oh, hey there, so this is where you spend your days when your patients can't find you." It actually didn't upset me to see him, because it confirmed that my instincts had been right.

So once again I was on a merry-go-round of seeing therapists and doctors. I wasn't connecting with any of them. I went to see a couple new ones and told them the whole story. My illness was now on a whole other level. I had been taken off a very visible TV show, been all over the *Enquirer*, and forced into the hospital by Warner Bros. It was a lot for some of these psychiatrists to hear or want to deal with.

I felt so hopeless because any time I told them what had happened to me or what I had done, most of these new doctors seemed shocked. *I can't believe it...Oh, my God...*that kind of a reaction. I didn't honestly think my story was all that shocking. By this time I had left my old therapist, the one who had done nothing to help me. He never should have held onto me as a patient as long as he did, because he was not an eating disorder specialist. The one helpful thing he ever did was eventually tell my dad about Dr. Strober at UCLA. It was almost an afterthought. Just sort of in passing. After my dad told him he was losing me as a patient, he said, "Oh, there *is* this doctor, he's the head of the eating disorders program over at UCLA, his name is Dr. Michael

Strober." My dad was as angry as one can feel. He said, "You couldn't possibly have told me this a year ago?"

Sometimes I believe that having some sort of a "name" and money can be detrimental to recovery. I believe some doctors hold on to those patients who can pay without any further thought, and I'm afraid my old psychiatrist was one of them.

So my dad and I made an appointment to meet with Dr. Strober. We sat and talked for three hours the very first time we met with him. I was adamant that I would not go back into an inpatient program. I was never going back there again. I was over eighteen, so no one could really force me to do it, either. My parents felt that whatever Dr. Strober said would be OK—if he felt he could help me without hospitalization, then they would go along with that.

At that first meeting I convinced him that I would do all the work I needed to do, but I needed to live in my own house. And in talking to me for those few hours that first day, he made the decision that if I would come in every day he could monitor me closely enough and I would not have to be admitted to the hospital. I swore that I wouldn't miss one appointment or ever be late, as long as I didn't have to be an inpatient again.

I also spoke to him about my tremendous fear of having someone else see the number on the scale. I asked if there was any way he could treat me without weighing me every day. That was a big, big thing. I have always been afraid of weight. I'm always more "free" when I'm not on a scale. Even at that moment, I felt that if I could get beyond weighing myself on a scale every day I'd have won a small victory. I said, *Look, I weigh myself every day. If I have to be weighed every day all I'll do is focus on the numbers and you seeing them and judging me.* My explanation was good enough for him.

As my dad and I drove home from his office that first day, he looked over at me and said, "I think you're in good hands." I think he only half-believed it. But hope was our best option. We put our faith in the fact that we had found the right doctor, the right treatment, *finally*. We had a ray of hope.

Chapter Nine

Baby Steps

I started therapy right away, and it was a tremendous relief. Nothing I said shocked or surprised Dr. Strober. And he didn't start right off saying, "OK, I want to see ten pounds on you in two weeks," which is the hard-line approach they take in hospitals that scares anorexics to death.

When you're an inpatient who is drastically under-weight they pick a number and put an IV in you until you hit that number. Sticking an IV in your arm and letting you go four weeks later after you've gained enough weight to make everyone comfortable again is only a Band-Aid, barely touching the surface of the real issues. When that happens the girls are so freaked out because they feel so uncomfortable in their bodies, they'll do whatever it takes to lose the weight the minute they get out of the hospital. Dr. Strober had compassion. He never got angry with me; he worked with me to overcome my problems. He didn't look at me like I was a freak. Slowly, we took small steps. *Baby steps*. If you do the work inside, the outside will follow.

Altogether I was off the show for three weeks. I was able to return to the set to shoot the very last episode of *Growing Pains*. I had only the final week of rehearsing before shooting the last show. There were flowers and 'welcome back' signs waiting for me when I returned, and everyone was very concerned about me. It was so sad, considering how happy I had been there for so many years.

The last show ended with all of the cast members sitting around eating a pizza. If you watch the last episode it's obvious that I was only pretending to eat, though I did my best to make it look real. There was no way I could have taken a bite of pizza at that point. You might as well have pointed to a rat and said, "Go ahead Tracey, take a bite." A producer walked down from the audience and asked during rehearsal, "Can't you just take one bite? It's not looking real." I just shook my head. No, I couldn't. People still didn't get it. Nobody understood—if I could have taken a bite of pizza I wouldn't have been in this situation in the first place!

Roby was sitting up in the audience too, and he came down to tell me, "Do *not* do anything you feel uncomfortable with." So I faked my eating, and you can tell I was faking my eating. There was no other option. This was my reality.

My therapy schedule was very intense—five days a week, an hour or an hour and a half each day, for more than a year. Being removed from the show and hospitalized had triggered a huge outbreak of publicity. *TV Guide* was the first to print an article saying I would be off the show for a while due to anorexia nervosa. Then it was all over the tabloids—I was on the cover of the *Star, National Enquirer, Globe,* you name it. They were saying things like I was wasting away, unable to walk. I was living in a fishbowl.

People magazine approached my father just a week after I got out of the hospital and told him they were going to do a story on anorexia and planned to feature me. They requested an interview, and after a great deal of consideration I decided to cooperate. They were going to do a story on me with or without my participation, and I didn't want them to reprint the lies that were all over the tabloids, a lot of sensationalistic deathbed kind of stuff. I wanted a chance to speak for myself if they were going to write about me anyway—I needed to have my voice heard. After I did the interview they requested a photo shoot. They promised to be very discreet, which they were. They just wanted a headshot.

No body shots. This disease I'd had for two years and tried to keep secret was now on the cover of the magazine I bought every week. I thought it was a very fair and balanced article. They were very sensitive to me and the whole subject. But still, it was so bizarre to be going through something so personal, and be faced with my waning smile on the cover of *People* at every newsstand and checkout counter I passed.

That cover story really turned me into the face of anorexia. I was constantly in the tabloids. At one point Roby and I went to the premiere of a movie. Roby has a very bad back (he underwent major back surgery in 1990) and a picture was taken of us where he was leaning on me because his back was killing him. And they printed this picture in a tabloid saying something like "Boyfriend Roby Has to Carry Weak Tracey Gold." When really I was supporting him! The *Enquirer* was printing stuff like "Tracey was curled up in her bed in a fetal position, barely able to walk." Meanwhile I was driving myself back and forth to the doctor every day. I was sick, yes, but I was capable. That's the truth of anorexia: you can be a walking skeleton but still function through life. I tried not to drive myself crazy reading all this stuff. I knew I had put myself in this position.

I got so much publicity in the tabloids and with the *People* cover that I was approached by *Prime Time*

Live. They wanted to do a documentary on my illness and recovery. They didn't want to air it right away, they wanted to chronicle the battle for one year. Their plan was to give me a video camera and have my family pick it up and film me whenever I wanted to talk.

I was very against the idea when it was first presented, which is the way I kind of am with everything in my life. I hate every idea originally presented to me, no matter how great. Eventually I decided to go ahead with it, but I must have backed out of it twenty different times over that year, which of course, I was always free to do. My dad filmed me at various times over the year and three different times producer Shelly Ross came out to formally interview me. It was an ongoing project.

As spring turned into summer in that first year of recovery I wore my loose, sleeveless, baby-doll dresses that were so popular in the early nineties. I remember my parents said to me one evening, "You should put a shirt over your dress." They always begged me to wear sleeves in public. I said, "No, it's July. I'm fine, I'm not going to see anybody," and went out the door in my sundress and my bare arms. Of course as I walked into California Pizza Kitchen to pick up my dinner, a group of people from *Growing Pains*—my friends—were sitting there having a meal. I did feel self-conscious, like, *Why didn't I throw a shirt on,* because they were looking at me, and looking at each other, and they knew I wasn't getting any better.

There was a terrible conflict going on inside me. My brain was in a constant battle. Parts of me were embarrassed, but other parts of me were proud that I was so skinny. A big part of me was fighting to get better, and at those times I felt very self-conscious, on display.

I had taken a year off from acting to concentrate on getting better. Therapy was my full time job—and it was the toughest job I ever had. Dr. Strober did family therapy with my parents and Roby. My sisters even came a few times. But it was really my parents and I who had to come to grips with a lot of baggage. There were some heavy sessions with yelling and screaming. There was a lot of anger and fear and hurt feelings, but there was also healing.

The fact that I had such a close, tight-knit family certainly fed into my anorexia. The anorexic is usually labeled the "sick one," but I believe she's the one who is symptomizing the problems of the entire family. My family, as wonderful and loving as it was, was too close. There were no boundaries.

When I got really, really sick my sister Missy also lost a lot of weight at that point. She never had anorexia, but her weight dropped considerably, to the thinnest she'd ever been. We were not getting along at all during that time. She was extremely mad at me when I was sick. She had very little tolerance for my illness (which I now understand). We had always been best friends, but not anymore. When you're that sick you alienate everyone—even your best friend, even your sister. I was so wrapped up in my eating disorder that I didn't have time for anything or anyone else. Missy was hurt and mad; she had lost her best friend. I simply wasn't there... when you're starving you can't have a real relationship.

My dad and I became increasingly isolated from each other during this time. He was frustrated and only knew how to express his fear through anger. He could never get beyond the belief that the idea that the body was like a car and all I needed to do was fill it with gas (food).

With Dr. Strober we were all getting into "good" therapy. By "good" therapy I mean we were talking about the real issues. Bad therapy, in my opinion, is when you can skirt around the real issues and the doctor lets you slide and talk around the problem. I'd had plenty of that with my other psychiatrist, the one who let me go on and on about the easy stuff: light things, all the things that really aren't the issue, like what I ate that day. A doctor doing good therapy is tough, he knows what the issues are that can't be avoided. He's there to make you talk about them and get into them with you; he's there to bring them to the surface and air them.

My real issues were control and insecurity. I was an extreme people pleaser. The problem with people pleasing is that for many years I got rewarded for it but towards the end I started to feel drained. I felt like I wasn't being appreciated; I was being taken advantage of. I resented that people were taking advantage of me; and I resented myself even more for not standing up for myself. A lot of it was the way I was raised. When you're a child actress you learn early to behave on the set. Your voice doesn't count.

But this was years later and I was desperately ill. I was an adult and I didn't have my parents on the set to stand up for me, or a teacher or a social worker. Now I had to learn to stand up for myself, and I couldn't. It took so long for me to realize that when you stand up for yourself it doesn't mean the other person is going to hate you forever. You just do it, it's your right. No one is going to do it for you.

Another valuable lesson I learned is that if you do things for other people and expect to get something in return you will be continually disappointed. Only do things for yourself if they make you feel good.

Dealing with all this kind of stuff was painful. Six months into therapy with Dr. Strober, I hit rock bottom. In August there was a life-defining moment at Roby's apartment. I got up in the middle of the night. I couldn't sleep. I was still throwing up, taking diuretics, losing weight, you name it. I looked straight on at my body in a mirror and I was shocked. My heart was racing. I was at the lowest weight I had ever hit. I had a moment of seeing myself the way I really was, which was "death."

My heart pounded so hard I could almost see it beating in my chest. I was sure I was going to die. I thought to myself, *I am going to die tonight. Please, please let me just make it till morning.* Yet the worst part of it all was that I knew there would be no need for an autopsy. All anyone had to do was look at me and they'd know why I had died at age twenty-two. Shaking, I crawled back into bed. Trying to calm myself down, I told myself over and over that I just had to make it through the night. *I'll get better, I promise!* I prayed.

When I got up the next morning I talked to Roby and my parents. We went over to my parents' home and I went on camera to say that I was finally at the end of my rope with being sick. I wanted to be strong and beautiful. I wanted to have courage. That was more enticing to me than being "sick girl." I told them, *"I'm going to get bet-*

ter." And I meant it. That was the turning point. They all sensed that something in me had shifted. I never lost another pound after that terrible night. In truth it took a long time to reach a "goal weight," but weight *loss* stopped. That was it. I'd finally had it with my illness.

Even I was forced to admit that the number on the scale had gotten ridiculously low. Any idiot could see that it was dangerous. I also knew that every day I got on the scale I was looking for that number to go down lower. If it stayed where it was or went half a pound higher my whole goal was to knock it down again. Just playing that whole stupid game finally scared me so much, I just couldn't bring myself to do it anymore. I realized that no number would ever be low enough.

Over the rest of the year I slowly started to get better. I wasn't necessarily gaining lots of weight, but my whole attitude had dramatically changed. The cloud was starting to lift. I think I gained a couple of pounds, which was huge for me. I was still so fixated on the numbers that every pound I gained and could stay comfortable with was a major victory. Recovery is an agonizingly slow process. The first step was to try not to lose weight. The second step was to try to stop throwing up. The third step would then be to stop being so restrictive and ritualistic. More baby steps.

Breaking all of my complicated food rituals was a large part of getting better. Anorexia nervosa often goes hand in hand with OCD (obsessive-compulsive disorder). I've always had some OCD traits—weird things I would make myself do, like touching a doorknob three times, because if I didn't I feared something bad would happen. What, I didn't know, but I wasn't taking any chances. Or I would worry all day, thinking, *Did I turn off the iron before I left this morning?* With anorexia, these kinds of compulsions are magnified, to the point where I had become paralyzed by my fears. Dr. Strober put me on Prozac to take the edge off this kind of behavior.

I had so many rituals and habits that drove me (and the people around me) nuts that I had to undo. For years I'd had this thing where I would put my food in the microwave and overcook it. I would order my meal from a restaurant, pick it up, and when I got home put it in the microwave for fifteen solid minutes. Then, if I didn't stick the food back in the microwave for a little more nuking, I could maybe start eating. By the time I actually ate, the food would be all dried out and crunchy. I liked it that way. I don't know why, maybe because it prolonged the time I could actually eat. I always preferred things overcooked to undercooked, but this was far beyond any normality. There were many nights where I'd overcook my food to the point where my dad or Roby would look at my burnt food and say, "You cannot possibly eat that. I'm getting you a new plate." And I'd panic, because then I'd have to go through this whole process again.

Cutting down the microwaving time from fifteen minutes to ten minutes was a big step. Another thing I had to work on was that I'd get up in the middle of my meal and re-microwave it, because I dawdled so much over my food that it got cold. So I'd cook it again, bring it back to the table, dawdle over it some more, re-heat it again, and so on. It drove everyone crazy. Just to break all those patterns took a very long time. Recovery was a long, long road.

Chapter Ten

A Growing Resolve

I continued to go to therapy and *slowly* but surely get better through the fall. In January, after almost a year of therapy, I was offered a part in a television movie called *Labor of Love: The Arlette Schweitzer Story*, starring Ann Jillian. It meant going on location to North Carolina. I was anxious to get back to acting, because I hadn't worked for a year. My year off was the first break I'd had from work in eighteen years—since I was four years old. My parents and Roby were worried about my doing it, but I felt I could handle it. I had to start moving away from the "sick me." My mom came with me on the trip so I wouldn't be alone. I was still very underweight, but I got through filming and didn't lose any more weight while I was shooting. A huge accomplishment.

One night in North Carolina my mom got furious with me because I wouldn't eat a banana. My illness had upset my mom so much. We had gotten through some painful moments in therapy. It was time for her to face the fact that she had a serious problem herself. She was still throwing up, even when I was in the deepest depths of anorexia, and she knew I still threw up. It wasn't hard to figure out. She'd say to me, "Are you throwing up?" I'd toss it right back at her, "No, are *you*?"

Like I said, it had never really been hidden when I was young, though as I got older and eventually became sick, she got a bit more secretive. Her throwing up for a long time was out in the open. She had grown up in an era where throwing up because you were full was commonplace and had no name. There was always some excuse like her dinner made her sick. Or she ate too much. That kind of thing. She'd come out of the bathroom with her face puffy and her eyes red, whereas I went to great pains to hide what I was doing.

But that night in North Carolina was a critical moment for her. She was so upset with me for not eating, and I was so frustrated, that in a burst of anger I shoved the banana in question in my mouth just to show her I could do it. Then later that very same night I caught her sneaking off to throw up! We were on top of each other in a little apartment; there was no way she could deny it. She was mortified, but I know this scene played a big part in her decision to finally stop. It wasn't the last time either one of us threw up, but it marked another huge turning point.

* * *

Diane Sawyer came out to the house and did her personal interview with me and my parents and Roby to wrap up the *Prime Time* special. At the time of our final interview, a year after I had entered therapy with Dr. Strober, I had come a long way, though I knew I still had a long way to go. However, the tide had definitely turned, and the time was right to air the show, as I was doing well in my recovery.

The *Prime Time Live* special aired in May. The whole family gathered at my parents' house to watch it. At the very end of the special Diane Sawyer closed with the words, "As this segment airs on the West Coast, Roby Marshall is so sure that Tracey is on her way to recovery that he will propose to her." I couldn't believe my ears; I was absolutely shocked. My mom had been so nervous all night because we had friends and family on the East Coast and she had been afraid that somebody would call and ruin the surprise.

It was the most romantic proposal imaginable. Roby had already taken my father out to lunch and formally requested my hand in marriage. With permission happily granted, he had the ring ready to slip on my finger as the show aired, with my whole family there to share the moment, as he knew I would want. I couldn't have been more surprised—Roby is a very private person. I never would have imagined that something like this would have been his idea—right down to the exact words Diane actually said. It couldn't have been more wonderful. I felt like a princess.

Getting formally engaged gave me a great boost. It was yet another reason to want to get better. We set a wedding date for the following October. We always wanted to have a fall wedding, and five or six months wasn't enough time to put it together. I preferred to have too much time to prepare rather than not enough. You're only a fiancée once and a bride for the rest of your life.

Plus, I knew I needed the extra year to get healthier. Roby always said he would not marry me until he knew I could eat a bite of wedding cake at our wedding. He was absolutely serious about this. He told me, "I cannot and will not marry you unless I know that you are healthy enough to take at least a bite of cake." I said, "OK, no problem." I knew I had enough time to get there. I had my own plan in my head and my own goal I was working toward. Very, very slowly. I gained weight so gradually and over such a long period of time that I

Getting Better
– Summer 1993

Engaged – May
1993 – Yay!!

Dad and me –
working again

barely noticed it. I had plenty of time to get accustomed to each pound. More baby steps.

My life was moving forward in a very positive way. I was engaged, working hard in therapy, planning a big wedding, and looking for a new house for Roby and I to live in. During the year of my engagement my terrible, destructive eating patterns were getting slowly but surely better.

A year after I got formally engaged I was approached to star in a movie based on the true story of a girl with anorexia, *For the Love of Nancy*. I was, in fact, the *only* choice in the producers' minds. That's always what an actress wants to hear, but... I read the script carefully and knew I had to say no. I was still having such a rush of press at that time; I was still fighting the disease myself; I was really afraid of becoming the anorexia poster child. I didn't want to feel like I was using my illness to exploit myself and further my career. But more importantly the subject hit too close to home; it was too on the money. I just couldn't bring myself to do it.

The producers wanted badly for me to star in it, but again, this movie was going to be made with or without me, so they asked me to look at the script anyway and give them some advice on how to make it better. Once I got involved in it and started working with producers

Lloyd Weintraub and Vin DiBona, I started to come around. I knew I had to play this part. They were very open to my ideas, because they were kind, intelligent men. They were fathers, too, and they sincerely wanted to do a good job. It wasn't just another TV movie project for them; they really wanted to make it something special. I think in talking to me even back then, while I was still really struggling with my illness, I had an intelligent and honest way of expressing my pain. When I talked about my battle and why I felt I couldn't do the movie and the reasons why they needed to fix the script, they got very impassioned about the whole idea. I think I inspired them in the sense that they knew me, heard what I was saying, empathized with me and became more personally involved in the whole subject.

During the making of *For the Love of Nancy* I still didn't want to do any interviews with journalists where a meal or food was involved, because I knew that that would be the focus of the whole article: "Tracey ate two noodles followed by three cups of tea…" Though I wasn't ready to subject myself to such scrutiny, I wasn't one bit concerned about anyone's thoughts on what I did or didn't eat or how I appeared to anyone. I was still under a doctor's care, in really intense therapy. I took three weeks off from therapy with Dr. Strober to go do this movie on location in Vancouver B.C. I was confident in my recovery; I knew I was finally on the right path. If anyone else had a problem with it, that was their problem and not mine. I knew what I needed to do, which was eat the food my doctor and I had agreed upon. It was all very planned out and regimented in my mind. If it seemed weird to somebody else that was fine with me. I knew I was moving in the right direction.

I had completely made the commitment in my mind that I wanted to get better. During the making of this movie I turned the corner once and for all and stopped throwing up. This was a huge thing. Starring as an anorexic girl in this movie was kind of the nail in the coffin for this kind of behavior in my real life. How could I make this movie about anorexia and still be throwing up off-camera? It felt so wrong and dishonest to me. I didn't want to be a fraud. I wanted to really and truly recover. I wasn't making any pretenses about being any farther along than I was, but I wasn't going to go home after a long day of shooting this movie and throw up. It just wasn't an option in my mind. I was actually starting to feel a little pride in what I could do. Maybe I really could become a success story. Maybe I could even help or inspire some other girls.

Chapter Eleven

For the Love of My Boys

Being sick girl gets really old. I got a lot of attention for it. Too much. But people get tired of it quickly. It's almost like they will give you unlimited attention for a certain period of time. Then all of a sudden boom, you're supposed to be better, and by that time you're too deep into it to just stop being sick. You're suddenly supposed to snap out of it. It's just not that simple. You don't become anorexic overnight, and you don't recover overnight. A lot of people, and a lot of insurance companies, have yet to recognize this fact.

As the year and a half between my engagement and my wedding passed I graduated to once a week therapy with Dr. Strober. He is an amazing doctor, particularly helpful at the crisis point. He knows how to handle girls who are at the absolute depths of despair, hitting rock bottom. But by now I was very much on the right track. There was no doubt I still had work to do. I was still very restrictive about food and eating, and I still weighed myself every day. But I had done a lot of hard work, and I was confident that I wasn't going to relapse. I give Dr. Strober an enormous amount of credit for helping me. I'm a big believer in the benefits of therapy, but at some point you have to know when to stop. It can become a crutch. You have to be able to admit that you need help and go into therapy with an open mind, but you also have to know when to terminate.

Roby and I got married on October 8, 1994. It was the wedding of my dreams, absolutely amazing. My old castmates from *Growing Pains* all came, as did one of the show's producers, Steve Marshall. He had seen the *Prime Time* special on me and written me a very nice letter, saying he hadn't realized what I was going through and apologizing for not seeing the pain I was in as a result of his jokes. He asked me to save him a dance at the wedding. Of course I did.

I wore a Helen Benton dress that I had flown to New York to pick out at the Vera Wang store. Missy was my maid of honor, Brandy was a bridesmaid, Jessie was a junior bridesmaid and Cassie was a flower girl. The ceremony was held at a magnificent Catholic church in Burbank, and the reception was held in my parents' backyard. Roby and I then honeymooned in our favorite place on earth: Hawaii.

At last...

Mom and me

Brandy, one of my beautiful bridesmaids

Dad and me

The whole day was everything I wanted, and everything I could have ever dreamed about. Marrying Roby was the culmination of everything I had worked for. I wanted more than anything to be his wife, and I made it come true. *Yeah, me!*

We were living in a great new house in Studio City, and I threw myself into acting in movies of the week. I was very busy, doing a lot of traveling. After the wedding in October I started a new movie that December, then did three or four movies in a row immediately after that. I was establishing myself outside of Carol on *Growing Pains* and the girl with anorexia. I did a lot of work I was very proud of. I was becoming very successful and powerful in the movie of the week arena. My weight was very stable. I was doing great.

I had been happily married for a year and a half and everything in my life was going very smoothly. Because I had actually stopped menstruating for a year when I was desperately anorexic I was concerned that I might have a problem conceiving. I was terribly afraid that I might have damaged my reproductive organs. I had been warned of this possibility.

Roby and I had discussed parenthood, and I was really ready. I was on location in North Carolina shooting a movie when I caught the bug. All of a sudden I started

My Love

Keeping my promise

Soooo happy!

Perfect!

seeing pregnant women everywhere. Something went off in my mind: *That's it, it's time.*

Roby was much more nervous that I was. He asked me over and over, "Are you sure you can handle this?"

I said, "Absolutely, it's not like I'm gaining weight for no reason. It's weight so I can have a baby!" I was ready. I was eating properly, but still in a very restricted manner. I had my very particular breakfasts, lunches and dinners, plus certain snack foods I allowed myself. As usual they were all carbohydrates.

My doctor cautioned me that I probably wouldn't get pregnant my first month trying. Most women don't, even without a history of eating disorders. But I conceived the very first month. I was flying off the walls, I was so excited. I knew I was pregnant immediately. I knew my body so well, I was telling my mom way before my period was late that I was pregnant.

She would say, "Honey, it's not going to happen the first time you try. You just want it so bad."

And I said, "Nope, I'm definitely pregnant." And I was.

During my pregnancy with Sage I still didn't eat any dairy. It was one of my remaining phobia foods. I took calcium supplements instead. I was also still very afraid of being weighed at the doctor's office. My obstetrician, Dr. Pine, who I love, had been my gynecologist throughout my illness. Because he was aware of my history, he made a deal with me that I could weigh myself at home and report in each visit how much weight I had gained. Of course he could also visually monitor my progress. I did fantastically well, so not having official weigh-ins was never an issue. Dr. Pine is great... I will drive miles for him, so he can deliver my babies.

While I was pregnant I discovered some new foods. I had pea soup for lunch almost every day. My old favorites, like mushroom, I couldn't tolerate. I never had one moment of morning sickness or threw up, which was a great blessing for someone with my history. I was healthy as a horse. The only hard thing was giving up Diet Coke, which I quit cold turkey the moment I found out I was pregnant. It gave me an excruciating migraine as my body withdrew from caffeine, but it only lasted one day. It was the only day in my entire pregnancy that was hard.

I felt great. I didn't try to fight what was happening to my body. I said goodbye to all my cute clothes for nine months. When I was four months pregnant I hit a rough patch. I started to feel a little bit panicky. I was in a very awkward in-between stage where it was obvious I had gained weight but I didn't look particularly pregnant. I was feeling a little shaky, so I made an appointment with Dr. Strober to talk things over and touch base.

I had another doctor's appointment that day, where I was going to find out the sex of my baby. But I went to Dr. Strober's office first. And it was during that hour that I realized I really didn't need him anymore. We started to go over all the old issues, and I realized that I didn't *have* those issues anymore. I was just feeling a little fat, like most pregnant women feel at some point. It wasn't about anorexia. I wasn't about to start starving myself again. I was glad to realize this. I knew Dr. Strober's value, but I didn't have to depend on him anymore.

So I left there and went straight to the specialist who was going to perform an ultrasound. This was the point in the pregnancy where they could measure the baby, make sure he was growing, and be able to detect any problems. It was really just a side note that you learned what sex your baby was, but that was what I was really going for. I didn't think for a second there would be any problems. Roby and I went to the doctor's office.

While I was lying on the table the doctor said to me, "Do you want to know the sex of your baby?" And I answered, "Yes." So he said, "It's a boy." Very flat, no emotion. He had the personality of a wet noodle.

Then he said to me, "See this here?" pointing to the picture of the baby on the screen. "This is the neck, and it's measuring six. It should be measuring four. That is one of the key signs of Down's Syndrome. How old are you?"

Stunned, I answered "27."

He said, "Consider yourself 35. Because that's how likely it is that your baby will have Down's Syndrome. I'd like you to get dressed and go right next door and meet with a genetic counselor who will tell you everything you need to know. And I'd like to schedule you for an amniocentesis immediately. Today."

My breath was taken away. Roby and I were meeting my parents at the Ivy after this appointment to celebrate. The innocence of my pregnancy vanished in a second. We went to the counselors and they started showing us pictures in a book.

Then they said, "We'd like you to have an amnio right away."

And I said, "Uh-uh. No way."

It was lunchtime, and I couldn't reach my doctor. I wasn't about to do anything without talking to him first. Because they were recommending that I have amnio and I refused, they gave me a release to sign, to officially waive having the test. I signed it, and then sat down to read all the fine print, when Roby grabbed it out of my hand and said, "Don't read it. We're not having amnio, we're not sticking a needle in your stomach."

We didn't need it. At worst the results from amniocentesis would have prepared us for bad news. But we were going to love and keep our baby no matter what. It wouldn't have changed anything. So we left the office without having amniocentesis.

It was a real wakeup call for me. How could I have even been *thinking* about my weight? I was worried about how I looked, gaining a few pounds, and here I was being told that there was probably something terribly wrong with my baby. And the way I had been told! That doctor was so cold and nonchalant as he delivered the worst news I had ever gotten. It was at that moment I turned into a mother. I bonded with Sage fiercely right then. The love I felt for my unborn child was overwhelming. It knocked any concerns about weight right out of my head. The only thing my thoughts could focus on was my baby boy.

I had two other ultrasounds with other doctors, and the measurements that had concerned the first doctor turned out fine both times. But I had been shaken to my core. The rest of my pregnancy had a shadow of worry over it. Thankfully, everything turned out fine. I had an easy delivery and a perfectly healthy beautiful boy. A couple of days after his birth, after I had brought Sage home, I was trying to button the top button of his little newborn t-shirt and I couldn't, because his neck was too thick. I wanted to march right back to that doctor's office and show him my son and say, "Did you ever think to look over at my husband, you know, the man who was sitting right there in the room with us? The big guy, the one with the neck of a football player?"

I was extremely lucky. I had reversed the course of anorexia in enough time to prevent major damage to my body. My son was healthy. Having Sage was really the end of my anorexia. Every other concern pales in comparison to having a healthy child. To worry about what I weighed and what food I would eat that day seemed ridiculous compared to the thought of a baby who might not be born with every advantage life has to offer.

During my pregnancy I took good care of myself and did everything right. I gained exactly the right amount of weight for a healthy pregnancy. I never skipped a meal or ate anything unhealthy. I looked glowing and healthy the entire nine months. It was also nice that the whole time I was pregnant it never showed from the back—a blessing, believe me, I know. Up until the moment I delivered, if you saw me from behind you would have never known I was pregnant. I just had this huge stomach, like a giant basketball. Total boy.

Sage Gold Marshall was born on his due date: February 16, 1997. People don't realize that I gave birth to an 8 lb., 10 oz. baby, 21 inches long. He was a big boy—huge, actually. I was certainly doing something right to have such a large, healthy baby. You hear stories about teenagers not realizing they're pregnant until they're six or seven months along, or even giving birth without ever realizing they're pregnant. I don't get it. My stomach was *huge* at six months. Because Sage was so big I immediately felt very skinny after giving birth, just because I'd lost a lot of weight delivering him. I wasn't carrying my big baby around in front of me anymore.

In an especially touching moment, my sister Jessie was in the delivery room when I gave birth to Sage. She had very much wanted to be there; we had become extremely close during my illness. She had sometimes come over and slept in my bed with me to make sure I was still breathing when I was at my sickest. Sage's birth kind of brought us full circle, because I had been there when she was born; now she was there at the very beginning of my son's life. She was only twelve.

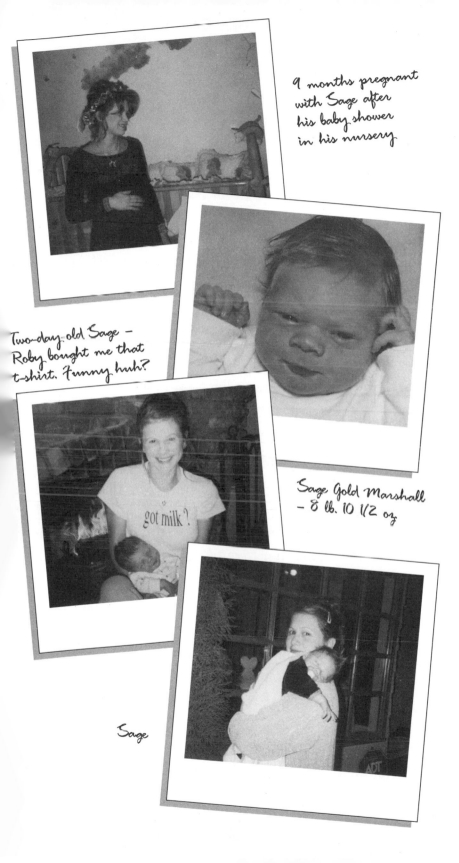

9 months pregnant
with Sage after
his baby shower
in his nursery

Two-day-old Sage —
Roby bought me that
t-shirt. Funny huh?

got milk?

Sage Gold Marshall
— 8 lb. 10 1/2 oz

Sage

After I gave birth there was never another thought that I could go back to anorexia. It wasn't about me anymore. Anorexia is a very selfish disease. Whatever I did to my body—to myself—would affect my children. Sage did not ask to be born to an anorexic mother. When I made the decision to become pregnant, I made the decision to say good-bye to my disease. I was not going to do something detrimental to my baby's health and well-being while I was pregnant, but also not after he was born. Living with him reinforces my decision every day.

I feel blessed in a sense to have had two boys first, because a mother's self-image so defines her daughters'. It's given me time to keep working on myself before having my baby girl. I've continued to make so much mental progress. After Sage was born I was still eating my special pasta. I was eating regular meals, and I was eating healthy food, but I still hadn't let go of some of my unhealthy preoccupations. I had a list of around ten meals that I could eat, and it always ended with pasta for dinner. I was still very much a restaurant person; I still found it easier to pick up my food rather than cook. That way I didn't know exactly what was in my meal. If it came from a restaurant I didn't see it being made, so I couldn't obsess about it. These quirks continued until I had Bailey, my second son.

I think mothers have the duty to provide the right example for their children (particularly daughters) concerning

Sage

Just pregnant
with Bailey

their bodies and food. Kids learn by example—I certainly did with my mom—and I want to project the healthiest image I can. A mother's issues about her weight will transmit to her daughter. Coming from a family of five girls, I'd worry about a girl so much more.

I love being a mother more than anything. I think motherhood was what I'd waited for all my life; it's what I was meant to be; the role that fulfills me. Sage was less than one day old when I said, "I want to get pregnant again; I want another baby." I was barely out of the delivery room! I loved *everything* about being pregnant. Even labor wasn't so bad—epidurals are a great invention.

Because my sister Missy and I were only fourteen months apart, the idea of having my kids very close in age appealed to me. My mother remembered very well how tiring it could be to have two babies, and then two toddlers. She urged me to wait, but Roby and I were both so madly in love with Sage, we couldn't wait to have another one.

Roby and I have a ritual on our birthdays. We go away together on the night before the birthday, usually to a hotel in the Los Angeles area, then celebrate with family and friends on the actual day. But the night before is just for the two of us. The year after Sage was born we spent Roby's birthday at the Malibu Beach Inn, which is the most fabulous, romantic hotel imaginable. It was simply beautiful, right on the beach. We were very happy and proud new parents and it was a wonderful birthday celebration. We went to Gerard's for dinner, where you feel like you're in Hawaii. We spent the whole time talking about having another baby. We decided we should start trying while we were on vacation in Martha's Vineyard. We were leaving the next week.

My parents and all five girls had planned this vacation trip back east. At the last minute Roby had to stay back at work and couldn't go, so Sage and I reluctantly went without him. It was a very long and tedious trip, three separate planes with a very lively one-year-old. I was terribly disappointed that Roby couldn't come, but I was happy that we'd had such a romantic tryst the week before. I consoled myself on the trip that we'd start trying for another baby as soon as Sage and I returned home.

Martha's Vineyard was heavenly. It was a great vacation. I was so relaxed that one night we were all hanging out after dinner and I said, "I want an ice cream sundae. Why don't we all go get some ice cream?" Since I had struggled with anorexia I had never eaten ice cream, not for years. But I had a sudden, intense craving for ice cream in a warm waffle cone...Everyone looked at each other, a little surprised to hear the words 'I want ice cream' coming out of my mouth. But no one wanted to make a big deal out of it, so off we all *ran* to get our dessert. It was delicious; I was glad I ate it. I chalked this very unusual event up to the eastern sea and air.

The trip home was a nightmare; we were all exhausted the way you get after a long vacation. We had a six-hour layover at one of the three stops and Sage was understandably cranky. So was I. I was complaining and irritable but finally realized that my period was due the next day. So I felt I had good reason to be a little out of sorts. But the next day came and went with no period. I'm as regular as a clock; I knew something was up. Just in case, I took a pregnancy test and sure enough, I was pregnant. Wow.

It was a practically identical pregnancy to the first one, which was great. I knew I was having a boy, I just knew it. Again, I never had any morning sickness. When the doctor confirmed that I was having another boy I was thrilled. When I was a little girl I was the most feminine girly daughter my mom had. She used to tease me, saying, "Tracey, you're going to have two boys, Rocky and Spike, and they'll be brutes. They'll outgrow you." Once I had Sage, I knew I wanted another boy. I wanted my boys to have each other like Missy and I had had each other.

Posing for
People magazine –
8 months pregnant

Sage and Mommy
at Bailey's shower

Bailey Vincent
Marshall
– 7 lb. 9 oz

My second pregnancy was smooth sailing. Even my delivery went easily. My water broke and I delivered five hours later, at 1:17 a.m. Bailey showed up two days before his due date. I happened to have had my hair colored the day he arrived, so my hair was perfect when he was born. I looked fabulous in all the pictures, which of course was very nice. Bailey Vincent Marshall has good timing. On March 4, 1999 he entered this world.

When I brought Bailey home Sage had just turned two. He was so excited, wearing his T-shirt that says "I'm a big brother." They're best friends and it makes me so happy...it reminds me so much of me when I was a child.

After Bailey was born some people asked me, "Aren't you disappointed? Didn't you want a girl this time?" Not at all. I know I'll have my little girl some day. And if I wind up being the mom of four boys, I'll be a very lucky lady. Roby and I have always known that we wanted lots of kids. There's plenty of time for a girl. Boys are amazing—I've turned out to be a great mom for rowdy little boys. My mom was right: I have two little bruisers. They're big boys, they look just like Roby—his little "Mini-me's." I'm the princess in my house, and I love it.

Meema, Aunt Cassie,
Baby Bailey and me
- 3/4/99

Bailey & Mommy
- 3/99

Bailey

Bailey

Chapter Twelve

Making Peace

When my sons were babies I was still very active doing movies of the week. Whenever I could, I brought them with me on location. Sage came to Montreal with me when he was only three months old. He also accompanied me to Vancouver on a shoot before he was a year old. When Bailey was six months old I did back-to-back three-week shoots in Utah and brought them both with me. I loved having them around. I couldn't have done it without them.

When we were home I was very caught up in being a stay-at-home mom. All those everyday sort of mom activities: cooking meals, playing games, giving them baths—I loved every minute. In 2000, eight years after the show went off the air, I was invited back to do a reunion of *Growing Pains*. One of the original producers, Mike Sullivan, had gotten together with one of the original writers on the show, David Kendall, and together they had come up with a new script. They approached all the actors with it. I was very wary—I probably had it for a week before I could bring myself to read it. I was afraid it would be bad. But it was a good story, very true to the characters. I liked it—really liked it. All the other actors did too, apparently, because we all reunited to shoot *The Growing Pains Movie*.

Though I was scared about going back, it was a tremendously healing event and a very positive experience overall. In the beginning doing the show had been such a dream come true. As a kid, I had idealized the whole experience in such a way that it almost *had* to crumble a bit. It wasn't as perfect as it looked—nothing is. And I didn't know how to handle it. The first years had been so great, and the ending had been so painful. I couldn't take a balanced view of the whole experience. I had loved *Growing Pains*, then hated it. I could find no middle ground.

Getting back together with everyone I realized again what tremendous chemistry the whole cast had. There had been, and still was, a great connection. It was very empowering to go back as a wife and mother, having had a successful career after the show ended. I was a whole, grown-up individual, healthy and strong, full of knowledge and experience. I was happily married and the mother of the two most beautiful little boys, who

Growing Pains reunion – Chelsea, Me, Alan, Kirk, Jeremy, Joanna and Ashley

came on location with me, as always. It was an oppor-tunity to make peace with all the cast members. It was great to see everyone.

I think they were all surprised at my transformation. I wasn't a little girl anymore. I had always been known for being very gullible, someone who would fall for any-thing. It was just like a real family where everyone had their role, and mine had been the wide-eyed, naïve, inexperienced daughter. That little girl was long gone. It was very healing to see everyone as an adult and finally put all the pain behind me.

*   *   *

Today I have a very active life as a mother and an actress. I still hate to formally exercise, but since I have a two-story house and two very active boys I get all the exercise any one person needs. I'm constantly running up and down the stairs and carrying my kids around. Nowadays I sit down with Roby and eat my meals. The boys aren't quite at the "big-people" food stage yet, so I usually wind up feeding them while I'm cooking our meal. But I sit down for dinner with my husband every night, and I eat what he's eating.

This is a minor miracle after all the years I spent ordering my meals from restaurants. For so long I'd cook for him and order my pasta from California Pizza Kitchen. It got tiresome, not to mention expensive: the meal, plus delivery and a tip every night. The restaurant people loved me: Every year I got Christmas cards. I was their best, most reliable customer for years and years.

Thank God I'm past all that. I also make a real effort to be open-minded about what my kids eat. I don't want to deprive them of all the fun stuff. I think if you're too vigilant and deprive your kids of sweets, they'll develop a sweet tooth later in life. They'll go on a junk food binge as soon as they can get loose. "Everything in moderation" is my motto.

My Boys

Mommy and her boys

I have three sisters who are much younger than Missy and I—currently aged twenty-five, seventeen, and fourteen. Of course I can't help but worry about them a little. But they saw so much of what went on with me that they have a good head on their shoulders about it all. My mom and dad treat them differently than they treated Missy and me because they've learned a lot too. After seeing what I went through with my illness, they don't talk about weight with my sisters. They don't make remarks about putting on a few pounds or say anything remotely critical about my sisters' body size. I'm so glad for my sisters.

Roby has also learned a lot. He's a swim coach, and he's much more aware of what he should and should not say to girls he's working with. A young girl's self-esteem is so fragile. Nine times out of ten you're better off not mentioning that a girl has put on some weight. Everybody's body is different—we all develop at different stages. Not everyone is meant to be a size two. A sixteen-year-old girl is already hyper-aware of her body. She doesn't need her coach telling her anything. A *male* coach in particular.

I still remember the director on *Growing Pains*, a Brooklyn guy, always battling his weight himself. He'd say to me, "If you'd cut out all that Diet Coke, you'd lose ten pounds in a month, I guarantee you." He was always full of helpful diet hints, courtesy of his ultra-skinny wife and daughter. I've never forgotten that comment. I mean, he actually spent time thinking about this, ways for me to lose weight? It seems to be a guy thing. They think nothing of saying things like, "You could lose ten pounds easy and look so much better." They'll throw a number on you. And he would always talk so loudly, everyone could hear what he had to say. I was so embarrassed. But this kind of stuff happens all the time in high schools, colleges, everywhere. An adult can be hurt by a comment like this, but a teenager can be crushed. I mean, they take it to their very soul. They can't see the situation clearly.

I get recognized a lot for many things, and it makes me happy. It's a great thing that I've been able to help *anyone*. I'm really proud of it. I think to take something bad and turn any part of it into something positive is the best you can hope for when you're faced with a situation like this. I'm proud of what I've done. Would I have chosen to be so well-known because I had anorexia? No, never in a million years. No one would choose this. But you have to play the hand that you're dealt in life, or deal yourself. I'm very pleased with the way I've handled my life.

Some things never leave you. Certain little quirks from the anorexic mindset stay with you no matter how many years pass or how well you're doing. A perfect example of an "anorexic moment" is when someone comes up to me and says something like, "I thought I recognized you, but you look so different now!" "Different" to them means "better," that is, more beautiful, older... not different FAT.

People mean well, but my brain hears that word "different" and my immediate first thought is "She means 'fatter.' She thinks I look *fatter*." My rational brain kicks in after a minute and I tell myself, "Put it out of your mind. Different means better, not fatter!" And I move on. But this is the way an anorexic brain works. Any comment like that, no matter how innocuous, can be taken the wrong way by an anorexic—even a recovering one.

Even after years of recovery, I think my brain will always work this way. I've had to literally retrain myself to stop from reading into things. I know where this kind of irrational thinking comes from, and I can short-circuit it right there and move on. It's not like the days when I was so sick. Back then I would interrogate people. If someone told me I looked good I would grill them for ten minutes: "What do you mean by 'good'? Does good mean fat? Do I look fatter than I did yesterday?" That kind of obsession is useless and never-ending. Now I don't obsess over a random remark for hours—just a few minutes. And I can go on with my day and my life.

I can sympathize with people who live with anorexics. Talking to an anorexic is like walking through a mine-field. You have to be so careful with every word you say, because most anorexics are incredibly sensitive to every nuance of every word that has anything to do with appearance or food or eating. Just a few months ago my mom and I were having lunch. I had had a really busy morning and was so hungry. I started eating eagerly the minute the food came to the table and my mom looked over and said "Tracey! Slow down, there's no need to shovel it in." I hadn't realized I was eating so fast. Her words just stopped me cold. "Mom!" I protested. "You just embarrassed me so badly! You made me feel like a pig!" My mom was taken aback. "I'm really sorry, honey," she said. "I didn't realize how that would sound. I just didn't want you to eat so fast you'd feel sick." It was OK, the feeling passed, but I felt like I had to speak up. Again, I'm so far along in my recovery now, and yet this kind of moment still happens. I think moments like this happen for all anorexics, no matter how recovered we get. Thank God I only notice them in passing now. There was a time when I wouldn't have eaten for days if anyone had said something like that to me.

I still struggle with obsessive thinking and compulsive behavior. Though I'm not crazy about medication in general, and am not a big believer in antidepressants, I continue to take the once-a-week Prozac pill, which has really helped to take the edge off. If you've got anorexia and the doctor thinks medication can help you, if you're really suffering and trying to figure things out, then it may be a good idea. An anti-depressant can help, especially when you're so deep into starvation that the serotonin in your brain has basically shut down and there's not much activity there. It can jump-start the process of the feel-good chemicals everyone needs and get you functioning again. But in the end I believe that therapy is the answer. Getting to the root of the issues that lead to anorexia is the best way to truly heal. Because anorexia nervosa is an *emotional* disease that affects certain types of personalities, you can't fully recover until you address those underlying issues.

Even today I'm still learning. What I've learned from my experience is that in our world it's much better to be a healthy, strong-in-mind-and-body, intelligent human being. There are more things I'd like to be than just "sick girl." When you have an eating disorder, it's a statement of not loving yourself. Your whole world is consumed with how people perceive you and what they're thinking about you. But you can never change what people are going to say about you and think about you. You have to know how you feel about yourself inside.

When you get really sick with anorexia you come very close to your own mortality. The problem is that when you're so young and you're so sick you think you're invincible. You feel like you can do whatever you want to your body and your body will take it because you're young. You'll make up for it later. All you're doing is losing weight... you're not doing drugs or staying up all night, so you don't think it's so bad. You can't really imagine that it's something you could actually *die* from.

I came to the point where I got smacked in the face with my own mortality. I really love life. I was never suicidal. I never thought, *I don't want to live. I hate this life.* It wasn't like I didn't want to be here. I did want to be here. Very much. So I chose to live a different way than I had—a happier, healthier way.

I look back on so many great things I did while I was sick with anorexia, like great vacations to Maui—my absolute favorite vacation spot, where I was so consumed with food. I wonder what those trips would have been like if I hadn't been so sick and obsessed. If I could do them over again when I wasn't so wrapped up in what I ate and didn't eat...

Look, I have body image issues like everyone else. Every once in a while I hear a little voice saying, *You should be thinner.* Or if I'm going to see someone I haven't seen in a long time, since I was anorexic, I worry about what they're going to think. When you recover from anorexia, people are going to comment on the way you look. That's just a constant fact of life. You have to be prepared. People don't know how to phrase certain things for our forever-fragile egos. When you're recovering you've got to remember that most people aren't as sensitive as you are. It's a key thing to realize that. Know where you are in the stages of your recovery and don't worry about other people's words and reactions.

Though I know that I am recovered, it's something to keep a check on. Anorexia is definitely my "Achilles heel." Everyone has a weak spot and this is mine. The good thing is, I'm far enough away from the whole experience not to ever go back to where I was because I have two children; two lives I'm responsible for. They need me. This is not to say that I don't have bad moments or that I don't have to be more careful than other people. But overall, I've really got a lock on it. I've walked down that road before and I don't want to do it again.

I credit my boys with my recovery. Motherhood matured me. Any selfish aspects in your personality have to be erased if you want to be a good mother, and that's my goal in life. If I do only one thing well, I want it to be mothering. If I raise happy, healthy kids who want to come home for Christmas, I'll have lived a very successful life.

Every now and then I see someone who is clearly suffering from anorexia. The warning signs are very apparent to me because I've been through it, but it's important for other people to recognize the signs as well. I was at a restaurant the other day and one of the servers was so severely anorexic it was horrifying. It was disturbing for me to see. I was very glad that she wasn't my waitress. You'll find that anorexics like to be around food. They serve food and they cook food. They do this so they can flex their self-control and not eat while everyone else does. That self-denial is empowering to them. I remember.

I think things like this should serve as a real warning sign for parents. If your kids want to work at a cookie stand or an ice cream parlor or a bakery and they're getting skinnier and skinnier, or if they want to cook and prepare food for the rest of the family but they won't eat—these are classic symptoms. I cooked and baked for everyone when I was sick and never tasted a bite. It's that unhealthy mind process of being strong enough to deny yourself these things that people need to watch out for.

I was raised in a very close-knit, loving, hectic environment. It was a great, happy family, but being the oldest daughter, the first to grow up and break away from that cozy group, was a very scary feeling. Missy and I were raised the same way, to be "good girls," but my sister went all the way across the country to college and found her own voice. Missy is just a tougher, more defiant personality in general. She got her normal teenage rebellion stuff out of the way in college. You know, tattoos, that kind of thing. Now she's Melissa, a psychologist living in Maine, and Bailey's godmother. But she'll always be "little Missy" to me.

A support system is key to getting better. Almost always when you have someone who is young and gets sick with anorexia, there are family dynamics that need to be addressed; issues that need to be dealt with so the anorexic can get better. In my family, for example, my mom and I were too close. Intertwined, enmeshed. It's something to this day we still work on. And of course my mom had her own eating disorder. I was an extreme "pleaser": "Are you mad at me? Are you mad?" Constantly I would ask that question.

I know there are some parents who don't want to go to therapy. They'll say it's the daughter's problem. *She just has to eat!* They don't want to focus on their own stuff. When that happens it's time for the therapist to get tough, to ask parents, "Do you want your daughter to die? You need to get into therapy now."

It can be so many things. It's the mother/daughter relationship, the lack of control one feels and the need to control whatever one can. It's the role the girl has in the family—she usually plays the "good girl." I was good, to the point I think of being too good. It's OK to be bad once in awhile, to rebel a little. It's OK to talk back a bit. It's only normal, it's the natural course of things.

I feel I've finally found my true voice. I'm appropriately assertive. I speak up and don't let people push me around. I don't feel the need to be perceived as the "good one." You don't need to be a pushover to be good, you just need to be true of heart.

I never thought I'd be in a place to write a book like this. I'm still too young to write an autobiography at this point. This can't be the story of my life—I still have a whole life to live! But I learned some hard lessons early on that I wanted to share in my own words, in my own time, with you.

I remember that when I was sick I would always say that having anorexia felt like I was drowning. I would struggle to reach the surface and stick my hand up, waiting for someone to grab it and pull me out. Somewhere along the way, I realized that the only person who could pull me out was me.

We're only given one shot here, and we're in control of making it as good as we want or as bad as we want. Life will throw you curve balls. It's how you hit them that counts. You can show what you're made of by the way you deal with those "curves." I want to be known for being a great mother, wife, daughter, sister, friend. At the end of the day, it's not about the numbers on a scale, the size clothes you wear, or the food you did or didn't eat. It's about the quality of the life you lived.

Afterword

The Price of Recovery

The pressure to get better quickly—to just snap out of it—can add to the stress of the disease. Just recently I read a magazine article about an anorexic girl who committed suicide because she felt so guilty. Blue Cross wouldn't pay for her hospitalization, and years of illness had drained most of her family's resources. I believe her parents had some money, but I can sympathize that her guilt was overwhelming. I know that years of treating an illness like this can exhaust any family's budget.

I was so lucky that while I was sick money issues didn't place an additional burden on me or my parents. I could get the best help available regardless of its cost. I had trouble finding the right help, but paying for it was no problem. And it wasn't like I was taking up all my parents' money to get better. I spent my own money that I had earned. I look at girls who need help now and really worry. . . therapy, hospitalization. . . the expense is just outrageous.

It is up to the employer in 29 states to elect to have mental illness covered at all in their health insurance plans. Anorexia nervosa, bulimia, and in fact all eating disorders fall under the category of mental illness, so if your insurance plan doesn't cover mental illness, you're out of luck right from the start. SAG (Screen Actors Guild), my insurance, does not cover anorexia. It is no exaggeration to say that women have died from anorexia as a result of no insurance.

Even when a girl or her parents has mental health coverage in their insurance plan, the number of days for in-hospital stays is usually limited to much less than what's needed for her to get better. According to the Eating Disorders Coalition website, insurance companies routinely limit the number of days they will reimburse, which forces doctors to discharge patients with anorexia nervosa too early. According to a recent survey of eating disorder specialists, almost 100% said that their patients are suffering relapses as a consequence of managed care coverage limits. And virtually all specialists believed that patients with anorexia are placed in life-threatening situations because their health insurance policies mandate early discharge.

According to the American Psychological Association website, a Wesleyan University study analyzing the health insurance claims of 4 million people found that the average length of treatment, 26 inpatient and 16 outpatient days per year for anorexia nervosa, is much lower than the American Psychiatric Association's recommended standard of care. Think about it—16 outpatient visits a year for a girl suffering from anorexia. That's barely more than once a month!

Again, I was lucky, but it was a long, hard road I traveled, a journey I wouldn't wish on anyone. I believe that early, effective intervention and treatment is so important for people with eating disorders; and *preventing* them in the first place would be even better. I do think that if I had been correctly treated earlier, I might have been spared my long downward spiral and the nightmare of hospitalization. Because of this, I find it especially heartening that Senator Hillary Clinton has recently taken up the cause and sponsored, along with Senator Bingaman, the Promoting Healthy Eating Behavior in Youth Act of 2002. It recognizes that as far as eating disorders go, prevention is the best cure of all.

This bill is so important that I'm reprinting parts of it below. (Note that the first five bullet points specifically concern anorexia nervosa.)

To amend the Public Health Service Act to establish a grant program regarding eating disorders, and for other purposes.

Be it enacted by the Senate and House of Representatives of the United States of America in Congress assembled,

SECTION 1. SHORT TITLE.

This Act may be cited as the 'Promoting Healthy Eating Behaviors in Youth Act'.

SEC. 2. FINDINGS.

Congress finds the following:

(1) Anorexia Nervosa is an eating disorder characterized by self-starvation and excessive weight loss.

(2) Anorexia Nervosa is common: an estimated .5 to 3.7 percent of American women will suffer from this disorder in their lifetime.

(3) Anorexia Nervosa is associated with serious health consequences including heart failure, kidney failure, osteoporosis, and death.

(4) Anorexia Nervosa has the highest mortality rate of all psychiatric disorders. A young woman is 12 times more likely to die than other women her age without Anorexia.

(5) Anorexia Nervosa usually appears in adolescence.

(6) Bulimia Nervosa is an eating disorder characterized by excessive food consumption followed by inappropriate compensatory behaviors, such as self-induced vomiting, misuse of laxatives, fasting, or excessive exercise.

(7) Bulimia Nervosa is common: an estimated 1.1 to 4.2 percent of American women will suffer from this disorder in their lifetime.

(8) Bulimia Nervosa is associated with cardiac, gastrointestinal, and dental problems including irregular heartbeats, gastric rupture, peptic ulcer, and tooth decay.

(9) Bulimia Nervosa usually appears in adolescence.

(10) On the 1999 Youth Risk Behavior Survey, 7.5 percent of high school girls reported recent use of laxatives or vomiting to control their weight.

(11) Binge Eating Disorder is characterized by frequent episodes of uncontrolled overeating.

(12) Binge Eating Disorder is common: an estimated 2 to 5 percent of Americans experience this disorder in a 6-month period.

(13) Binge Eating is associated with obesity, heart disease, gall bladder disease, and diabetes.

(14) Eating disorders are commonly associated with substantial psychological problems, including depression, substance abuse, and suicide.

(15) Obesity is reaching epidemic proportions: 27 percent of United States adults are obese and 13 percent of children and 14 percent of adolescents are seriously overweight.

(16) Poor eating habits have led to a "calcium crisis" among American youth: only 13.5 percent of adolescent girls get the recommended daily amount of calcium, placing them at serious risk for osteoporosis and other bone diseases. Because nearly 90 percent of adult bone mass is established by the end of this age range, the Nation's youth's insufficient calcium intake is truly a calcium crisis.

(17) Eating disorders of all types are more common in women than men.

(18) Eating preferences and habits are established in childhood.

(19) Poor eating habits are a risk factor for the development of eating disorders, obesity and osteoporosis.

(20) However, simply urging overweight youth to be thin has not reduced the prevalence of obesity and may result in other problems including body dissatisfaction, low self-esteem, and eating disorders.

(21) Therefore, effective interventions for promoting healthy eating behaviors in youth should promote healthy lifestyle and not inadvertently promote unhealthy weight management techniques.

SEC. 3. PURPOSES.

The purposes of this Act are as follows:

(1) To increase preventive health activities designed to promote the development of healthy eating habits and behaviors in youth.

(2) To support research to develop and test education-al curricula and intervention programs aimed at promoting healthy eating habits and behaviors in youth.

(3) To identify and disseminate effective intervention programs aimed at promoting healthy eating habits and behaviors in youth.

Latest Major Action: 4/24/2002 Referred to Senate committee. Status: Read twice and referred to the Committee on Health, Education, Labor, and Pensions.

It is heartening to see that someone as influential as Hillary Rodham Clinton recognizes the seriousness of eating disorders as an illness and that prevention and early intervention and treatment are critical; and that she is working hard to make others recognize the same thing. When people stop treating anorexia nervosa and other eating disorders like bad eating habits, girls like the one in the magazine article will get the support they need to fight hard and win.

To my parents:

Harry Gold — you adopted me and raised me with unconditional love — no girl could have asked for a more wonderful childhood or a better man to call "Dad" — I love you.

Mom — You have shown me that to be a mother is the greatest gift on earth — thank you for being my mother and my friend.